'DON'T LOOK WALLPAPER'

THE KENNETH MCKELLAR STORY

SCOTLANDS GREATEST TENOR OF THE TWENTIETH CENTURY

by PETER CAMERON

Foreword by PROFESSOR GEORGE McPHEE OF Paisley Abbey

Dedicated to all those in Scotland and from all over the world, who loved the music and entertainment provided by Kenneth McKellar .

Proceeds from the book to Cancer Research UK

First published in 2011 by Linn Publishers
ISBN 978-0-9555837-1-1

Copyright Peter Cameron 2011

Printed in Great Britain by Clydeside Press Ltd
Glasgow

Contents

- Foreword
- Preface
- Acknowledgements

Foreword by Professor George McPhee

Kenneth McKellar is a household name. I first came across him through early albums of Scots songs which were frequently played at home when I was in primary school. I was later thrilled and honoured to work with him at Paisley Abbey in 1967 in the first series of recording sacred songs, leading to a life-long friendship. Kenneth was a true lyric tenor and a wonderfully intuitive and well-rounded musician who could turn his hand to composition, arranging and conducting. Above all he knew how to communicate and, whether with a Handelian aria or with a folk song from the Hebrides, he was able to gain the hearts of a world wide audience through his performances. He is a legend and a giant in Scotland.

Preface

I had known and appreciated the talents of Kenneth McKellar from his Radio and T.V. programmes 'A Song for Everyone'.

Shortly after his death in April 2010 I had listened to a programme on Radio Scotland entitled 'The Reel Blend' in which the programme presenter Robbie Shepherd met with Kenneth McKellar and went on a tour with him from Paisley Abbey to Largs and then to Dunoon.

I then wanted to know more about Kenneth so I asked Paisley Library for a copy of his autobiography or biography .
I was surprised to find that none existed, so I decided to do research with a plan of writing a biography. My research revealed that Kenneth had planned to write a book entitled 'Don't Look at the Wallpaper'. but never got round to doing so. As I researched I became amazed at the world wide appeal that Kenneth had.

I gained an insight into how popular Kenneth was when I called into a music store at the end of 2010. I looked in the Scottish section for albums by Kenneth McKellar, only to find that there were none in stock. He was the only artist to be sold out, at that time. The assistant indicated it might be a number of weeks before the Kenneth McKellar section would be restocked.

I was keen to have a copy of the album, the Songs of Burns and the Song of the Hebrides. I went online to order the album only to receive a reply that my order would be filled in two or three weeks. It took ten week before I received the album, however it was well worth the wait as the album was excellent.

Johnstone 2011

Acknowledgements

Joe Campbell formerly managing director for West Sound Radio in Ayr.
When I spoke to a friend who listened on a regular basis to West Sound Radio, to say that I was researching the life of Kenneth McKellar, He said 'You must contact Joe Campbell of West Sound Radio'. Joe was so helpful, he knew Kenneth and his family over many years, he was able to give me a 'rare' picture of the family and Kenneth in particular. I cannot thank Joe enough for his time, input and encouragement, and for being so patient in answering all my questions. Being able to visit with Joe in his home in Ayr was a delight.

Kenneth Spiers of the Paisley Daily Express
Kenneth had written various articles for the Paisley Daily Express at the time of Kenneth's passing and at his Memorial Service. Kenneth was most helpful in putting a request in his paper asking those who had memories of Kenneth to get in touch with me.

David Roberts - Formerly of the Museum Service Renfrewshire Council.
David provided photographs for the book, and he helped and showed interest in the book.

Reference Library Staff at Paisley Central Library.
The library had compiled an excellent file mainly containing newspaper articles, but also other memorabilia on Kenneth.

Glasgow Room staff at the Mitchell Library, Glasgow
The Glasgow room had a comprehensive file on the history of the Alhambra Glasgow. Copies of programmes from many of the shows were available at the Glasgow Room.

Professor George McPhee of Paisley Abbey
George took time out of his busy schedule to provide a
Foreword for the book. George had known Kenneth for many
years.

Andrew Dunn
Andrew Dunn is a Director of Kerr's Music Corporation
Limited. He was most helpful in providing advise and his
expertise on the Songs included in the book which were
reproduced with the permission of the copyright holders.

My Family
I wish to thank members of my family for their support,
encouragement and assistance , especially my wife Catherine,
my daughter Claire and my sister Mairi.

Chapter 1

Schooldays, Holidays and Relations

The Mc Kellar Family

Kenneth had two elder brothers, Harry now deceased, who was head of the metrological unit for Scotland and Jimmy now living in High Wycombe, who was a top chef in London. He also had a sister who died in infancy.

On the 27th February 2011, Kenneth's surviving elder brother Jimmy passed away. Jimmy had attended the memorial service at the Paisley Abbey in June 2010 and appeared in the BBC Alba tribute programme to his brother and friend Kenneth. As the two got older they became very alike in appearance but really very different in personality

When Kenneth was three years old his mother decided she didn't want her boys in a 'close' in the centre of Paisley. The 'close' is a local term for the access area for a large tenement building housing six to eight families.

Despite the fact that his father didn't want to move as he had born and raised in Paisley, Kenneth's mother Jean, won the day and the family moved to 6, Baronscourt Gardens in Elderslie. The house had just been built and was secured for a mortgage of £500 over 25 years.   The move took the family from a tenement flat in 12 Mary St., Paisley, where Kenneth was born. The Google Map of 2011 indicates that Baronscourt

Gardens is in fact at the west edge of Paisley, next to Elderslie.

Both Kenneth's dad Henry (Harry) and Grandfather Archibald ran a licensed grocers' shop at 72, Causeyside Street in Paisley. The shop was at the corner of Causeyside Street and Canal Street and was referred to as McKellars' Wine Shop and the business was established in 1874. However none of Harry's boys wanted to be a part of the business as they had other career choices in mind.

When Ken was asked if he came from a musical family he responded that his father and some of his father's brothers sang in the choir in the High Kirk in the Oakshaw area of Paisley. In 1990 plans for a merger with the other two Churches in the Oakshaw area which were known as the Hill Churches were discussed. The merger of the High Kirk, St. John's Church and the Congregational Church took place in August 1991.

<u>Don't Look at the Wallpaper !</u>

When he was just 3 years old, Kenneth had the old 78's of Nursery Rhymes and was able both to wind up the gramophone and change the records much to the amazement of the family. The family gathered a collection of Gilbert and Sullivan Operas and recordings by bass, baritone and tenors, to which the family enjoyed listening. There wasn't much Scottish music in the McKellar home as there wasn't much being recorded. There was also recordings by the great singers Caruso and Gigli and Kenneth 'lapped up this music' which was quite unusual for someone of his age living in the West of Scotland.

Harry McKellar recognised that from an early age his son could sing. When people came to visit the McKellar home, Dad always asked Kenneth to sing. He felt embarrassed, as did the visitors. His songs were from Paul Robson which wasn't exactly a suitable choice for a small boy to sing. Kenneth would stand and face the wall which led him in later life when he contemplated writing a book, which he never got around to doing, although he spoke about often. The title he had chosen for his book was 'Don't Look at the Wallpaper', which is the title of this book.

One wonders how this book would compare with the one Kenneth would have written .

Mrs Ward of Elderslie

The family had moved to Elderslie, and Kenneth would sing his Nursery Rhymes to a neighbour Mrs. Ward. Kenneth would wander over to her home for a cup of tea or a lemonade. Mrs Ward said one day she would hear Kenneth sing at the Albert Hall in London.

Years later Mrs Ward and her family moved to Chiswick in the London area, by that time Kenneth's singing career had taken off and he was to perform at the Albert Hall. Who was able to come and fulfil the

prediction she had made years earlier? As she listened
to Kenneth sing 'Hiawatha' at the famous Albert Hall.
she was thrilled.

To Primary School

When Kenneth was 5 years old in 1932 he went to
school at the John Neilston Institute (in the Primary
department, the school was in Paisley). Kenneth would
have taken a tram which passed not far from where he
lived and got off at the west end of Paisley and walked
down Well St., to the Primary department in
Underwood Lane.

Peter Stewart

A classmate of Kenneth's in Primary one was Peter
Stewart who in 2011 lives in West Brae which looks out
onto the main school building. Peter provided a
photograph of the boys in Primary two with Kenneth
wearing a kilt. Peter recalls that Kenneth wore a kilt
throughout the Junior school. Their first teacher was a
a Miss Marr and on the first day of school there were a
number of those entering Primary one, in tears. Until
1938 the John Neilston was a fee paying school and had
the reputation of being a very good school.

Peter tells that at 12 years of age Kenneth took part in a
presentation 'Who Killed Cock Robin' and he felt that
Kenneth enjoyed singing. Years later when Peter and
his wife May attended a Flower Show at the Templar

halls in Paisley, Kenneth was there to open the show. From a distance Kenneth recognised Peter and made his way over to greet Peter and his wife and both were impressed by his thoughtfulness on that occasion.

Peter left school at 14years of age to work in his father plumbing business, whereas Kenneth stayed on at school to gain qualifications to go to University. Peter always remembers being a classmate of Kenneth McKellar and has followed his career with pride and interest.

The Porridge Bowl

The main building of the John Neilston school on West Brae in the Oakshaw area of Paisley and was designed by a leading architect of the day, Charles Wilson and constructed between 1849 and 1852. The roof area has been described as an astonishing addition to Paisley's skyline, in the form of what the locals call 'The Porridge Bowl'. The central atrium contains a statue of a Greek philosopher Diogenes, by a local sculptor Alexander Stoddart. The school closed in 1989 and the name of 'The John Neilston' was no longer used. In 1991 the building the building was converted into flats. At night, this landmark building is enhanced by floodlighting.

Rita Fearns

Rita of Paisley had memories of Kenneth. Her father Peter Williamson was an engineer at Brown's brickworks and also tutored young people wanting to learn to play the violin/fiddle. The Williamson's lived in Fulbar Road, (known as the Chain Road).

Kenneth's mother was keen that he become a musician, so they would walk from their home to the Williamson's home so that Kenneth could receive tuition from Peter. Peter found that his pupil was not really interested in learning to play the violin/fiddle. In fact he seemed more interested in looking out at the Coats Mills wood yard. Much to his mother's disappointment, he showed no signs of becoming a musician at that time.

Peter Craig

Peter Craig was in a class above Kenneth at the John Neilston. He has lived in Paisley all his life. Both Peter and Kenneth were chosen for the Abbey choir when Kenneth was about 10 years old. He became a member of the Choir whereas Peter whose love was playing the fiddle, decided not to take part. Peter only met with Kenneth when they both went for rehearsals for the School Orchestra . Mrs McKellar wasn't prepared to let Kenneth off the hook as far as learning to play the violin. He took lessons and became competent enough to be chosen for the School Orchestra at the age of ten.

To a Concert in the St. Andrew's Halls

As part of his parents efforts to instil a love of music in their son, they took Kenneth to a concert in the St. Andrew's Hall in Glasgow, the Singer at the concert was the Italian tenor Beniamino Gigli. Kenneth was enthralled by Gigli's singing and, he considered he had not heard a more beautiful singer before. The exposure to music at home and having such an experience as listening to Gigli sing, helped to prepare him for a future career in music, and being to able emulate Gigli by becoming an exceptional Tenor.

Family Holidays to Inellan by Dunoon

Kenneth always got excited when the time came for the family to go to Inellan for the family holiday. The family took a house in Inellan which is just South of Dunoon. Besides the family, Harry's father and mother Archie and Margaret came along. The journey to Dunoon started at Gilmour Street station in Paisley. The train took the family to Gourock to the ferry terminal for Dunoon. It was usually an eventful journey and the family got excited as Dunoon Pier approached. A taxi ride followed to Inellan and freedom. While staying there Harry and the boys used to go out on a boat fishing for mackerel near Toward Point, while there father would sing the song "I wish a wee fishy would come, would come". Sometimes a wee fishy or even a big fishy would indeed come.

At the Bowling Green

While on holiday the evenings were spent at the Inellan Bowling Green. The midges were murder and there was a prevailing smell of citronella (a lemony smelling candle to repel the midges). Father wasn't bothered by the midges as he smoked a pipe. He smoked Condor Sliced which the midges did not like at all.

When Kenneth and his wife Hedy took their one year old son Kenneth to Inellan, Kenneth took part in a summer show at the Queens hall in Dunoon. He was the first performer to have a Summer show there in 1960. One of the highlights of his career was when the young family were approaching Dunoon pier and over the tannoy came his version of the 'Song of the Clyde'.

The View Point Largs

When visitors came to the McKellar home they were taken on a trip to Largs. In particular, visitors would be taken to the view point above Largs. Kenneth's opinion was that this view was one of the finest in the world, and this was based on visiting many parts of the world. From the view point the visitor can see such magnificent views as the mountains of Arran which dominate the skyline as the viewer looks southward. In Kenneth's words the view both north and south is awe inspiring and majestic.

The McKellar family would often visit Largs for a breath of fresh air. Largs was a place where Paisley folks often retired to, so when the family went for a short outing they always met some Paisley Buddies who had settled in Largs. Ken's uncle had a car and the family all squeezed in for a trip to the coast. A visit to the Moorings or Nardini's to buy some fish suppers and then make for view point.

To the Pictures

Kenneth and his brother Jimmy would look forward to Saturday mornings when they would take the tram ride from Linwood Road end, to the Saturday morning children's matinee at West End Cinema in Paisley. The cinema has been knocked down and a block of flats stands in its place. At that time Paisley had 8 cinemas running simultaneously.
Going East from the West End cinema, there was the Regal knocked down in March 2009.
The Palladium in the Weigh-house Close which was demolished to make way for the Paisley Centre Car Park after being a warehouse for a local furniture store. The Picture House, whose entrance way was used as the entrance to the Paisley Centre.
The La Scala was knocked down to make way for the Littlewoods store.

The Glen Cinema stood right in the Centre of the town at the cross. The entrance was where Harvey's the furniture store now stands. On 31st December 1929 one Paisley's saddest tragedies took place in the Glen Cinema at the afternoon performance. A canister of film started to smoulder causing smoke to enter the main cinema. In the panic to leave the cinema 70 children perished in their desperate attempts to escape.

The Astoria in Lawn Street became part of Arnott's store which displayed furniture, and was affectionately know as the Bug Hut.

The New Alex was at the South end of the town of the at the corner Neilston Road and Orr Street. Finally the Kelburn cinema at the east end of the town, now knocked down to make way for retirement flats, after being destroyed by fire.
The boys enjoyed James Cagney films, Kenneth watched 'Blossom Time on 6 occasions, starring Richard Tauber . Some cinemas would accept "jellie jars" (jam jars) instead of money to watch a film

Willie McCulloch

When asked was there music in his family, Kenneth mentioned Archie Anderson an uncle, who was one of the first artists in Scotland to make a record. Archie appeared on the stage in London musicals, he had a very fine baritone voice and he recorded an amount of Scottish material.
Another relative who had musical talent was Willie

McCulloch, a cousin of Kenneth's dad. Willie had recorded monologues on the Columbia label on '78s' , which became scratched and difficult to listen to. Decca asked Kenneth to record some of Willie's material and to imitate him, as he had a similar accent.

Willie would come into Harry's shop when Kenneth was there and say things like "I'm very sure of death, and I hope Kenneth keeps his heid and he'll get on all right." Harry would reply "Willie if you had lost yer heid, you might have got further."

Willie would entertain in the shop which always involved two old women talking. An example of the kind of patter they came away with.
"How's John today?"
"He's got a sore back."
"Who's he under?"
"Oh it's doctor McGregor."
"Its nice to know John's sore back is in the hands of a well kent face."

Another of Willies' monologues went as follows:
"I was just saying that Mrs Blue should learn to keep her tongue off her neighbours".
"A woman like me with a regulated mind , its disgraceful."
"She goes from hoose to hoose gathering clavers and gets her tea here and her tea there and tells in one hoose what she heard in mine."

"She clavers on and the clavers come on just like snaw on a djuck's back."
"I used to be sorry for her poor man till I heard he was stone deaf, and I says to myself, Providence is kind."

At the School Concert

Kenneth was really made to take part in a school concert in the war years. He sang Handel's 'My Lady' and 'My Pretty Jane', both in a baritone voice. There was also an opportunity to 'Do' The Messiah as Ken put it.

The music teacher also made Kenneth take part in what he called ' A Jock's Box' in which he sang 'Where Ere You Walk' and 'The Blue was on the Rye', again as a light baritone. During his time at school he and some friends formed a group featuring guitar, drums, and Kenneth on violin. These experiences were to stand him in good stead in the future.

Chapter 2

Finding His Voice in Aberdeen

To University

Kenneth gained sufficient qualifications by the end of his fifth year in the John Neilston Secondary School to allow him to be enrolled at Aberdeen University to study for a Batchelor of Science in Forestry. So he had to leave all that had been familiar to him for the past seventeen years and move on.

Do something with that Voice.

While studying at Aberdeen University Kenneth sang in the University Chapel Choir. On one occasion, one of the baritones in the choir said to Kenneth "You need to do something with this voice of yours". He took these remarks as a compliment.

You're a Tenor

When Kenneth appeared on the Television programme 'Face the Music' in 1975, he spoke of being in the bass section at the University choir. The suggestion was made that in fact that Kenneth was a Tenor and he arranged to see Will Swenson the Director of music at Aberdeen University. Will asked Kenneth to go and purchase three items of music. When he went to the music shop, in 1947 every town had a shop which sold sheet music.
At that time he didn't know of the registers of the human voice. He asked the assistant did the shop stock

the three pieces of music he was asked to get, the girl at the counter asked which 'key' did he want the music in, Low , Medium or High. He answered whatever you've got and he purchased the high key version of each song. When he did an 'audition' for Will Swenson, he had no trouble in singing the High Key version and Will emphatically stated "You're a Tenor, go and sing with the Tenor section".

Will Swenson guided him and when Kenneth began to realised the effort required to perform Oratorios such as St. Mathew's Passion, The Messiah, Mozart's Requiem, The Creation and the 'B Minor Mass'. He really started to study these great works and performed all of them with the University Choir as a Tenor.

The Caird Scholarship

Will was impressed enough to give Kenneth lessons and coach him through the Caird Scholarship which was a post graduate scholarship for music. Will encouraged and pushed Kenneth to take singing seriously at school he had looked upon singing as a really good hobby, but no more that that. To a measure to sing in front of people was a 'Jessie' thing to do.

The Dunecht Connection

When Kenneth was a Forestry student at Aberdeen University, he lodged in a farmhouse about a mile from the family home of Robbie Shepherd of BBC Radio Scotland. Robbie's home was in the village of Dunecht which lies on the Aberdeen to Alford Road and near to the Cowdray Estates. Robbie recalls that his father who was the 'Sooter', the village shoemaker said that Kenneth would occasionally come to visit his father's shop.

It is likely Kenneth would have been with the Forestry squad on the estates as part of his practical training. When the training finished he would have found accommodation in Aberdeen near the University. Robbie recalls that when they did the occasional show or broadcast together Kenneth would always bring up their 'Dunecht connection'.

First recording

Kenneth was asked to go for an audition with Herbert Wiseman who was the Head of Music for BBC Scotland. He passed the audition and shortly afterwards was invited to take part in a play by Jessie Kesson which was being produced by Elizabeth Adair. Kenneth played the part of a schoolmaster who sung to the children , the song he was asked to sing was 'Shenandoah'.

His first recording was made in 1947 at the Beechgrove studio in Aberdeen under the direction of Herbert Wiseman. Soon afterwards he travelled to Glasgow to sing with Ian Whyte and the BBC Scottish Symphony Orchestra.

In the same year he made his Radio Debut as the main Tenor in a production of a Scottish Opera from the 18th Century entitled 'The Gentle Shepherd' for the BBC in Glasgow. It had been written by the Scottish poet Allan Rarnsay, music was arranged by Cedric Thorpe Davie a Professor of Music at St. Andrews University.
He recalls, "I sang the Main Tenor part and it was very beautiful".

First Network Recording with the BBC.

The producer of Kenneth's first network broadcast for the BBC was Eddie Fraser, a well known and experienced producer. The broadcast was being shown throughout the United Kingdom, Eddie suggested that Kenneth wear the kilt. He had no kilt but he was able to borrow one from Alec Carmichael, a well known baritone who ran a jewellery shop in Largs. Before the broadcast the BBC took publicity photographs of Kenneth in the kilt. They then proceeded to use these photographs for the next fifteen years, somewhat to Kenneth's annoyance.

Chapter 3

Have Horse, Will Travel

With the Forestry Commission

In 1947, Kenneth graduated from Aberdeen University with a Batchelor of Science in Forestry and joined the Scottish Forestry Commission.   He became involved in a huge project to replenish trees as so many had been felled for the war time effort.

This was before off-road vehicles were available to assist in the Commission's work. Kenneth had to travel hundreds of miles on horseback to reach areas which were otherwise inaccessible. He travelled all over the country Aberfoyle, Dundee, Deeside and Birkhall, and from Forfar to Skipness drawing up plans for regeneration with Sitka Spruce , Larch and Scots Pines. Kenneth commented that hundreds of thousands of trees were planted.   He had seen them being felled and another crop growing and being harvested.

When he was sent to work on Deeside and Donside his brother Jimmy came to stay with him while he was working at Duras. The work was to survey the area and Jimmy was to observe and comment on the fact that during his work, Kenneth saw no one or spoke to no-one at all. Jimmy's comments were that such an existence would have driven him mad.

To Carradale

Kenneth was asked to go and work in the Mull of Kintyre. He lodged with a wonderful old lady Miss Tina Patterson who lived at Portrigh which is a little area in the village of Carradale. She had the most marvellous stories of folk tales and a great grasp of Scottish history. It was all so real and vivid to her that sometimes it seemed as if she actually had been there. She said wistfully of William Wallace " I was awfully vexed to hear what they did to him in London." Kenneth felt that it was there, where he picked up the love of Scottish folklore. When William Wallace was taken to London after a trial he was eventually hanged, drawn, and quartered for high treason.

In Carradale he was introduced to the Songs of the Hebrides. There was a choir in Carradale with a Mrs Carson as its conductor. She had studied with Marjorie Kennedy-Fraser, so she was able to instruct Kenneth on Marjorie's ways.

While at Carradale Kenneth made contact with the Campbelltown Ladies Choir with its conductor Jen Brown, who had also studied with Marjorie. He would travel to Campbelltown two to three times a week to have lessons with Jen Brown and learn a bit of Gaelic.

Kenneth's view was that as he put it "The Jury was still out." on Marjorie, as she had 'jazzed up' the Songs of the Hebrides.

Marjorie Kennedy-Fraser

Marjorie was one of seven Kennedy children who were all professional musicians. Marjorie became world famous as a collector and arranger of the Songs of the Hebrides. In 1882 she began to study Gaelic music and the language and to collect folk songs. She gathered a large number of Gaelic songs and published them in a number of volumes under the title 'Songs of the Hebrides'. Marjorie's music was usually presented with piano accompaniments.

Today her work is viewed with criticism and suspicion, although she must be recognised for her work to combine traditional with modern harmonic arrangements, and bring the material to a world stage. Despite the criticisms it is largely thanks to her that these songs have been preserved for our use today .

Scholarship to Royal College of Music, London

While at Aberdeen University Kenneth obtained a Scholarship to Royal College of Music in London. Those who sponsored him were Herbert Wiseman, Ian Whyte and Herbert Howells (who was an English composer, organist and teacher). Kenneth's feeling was that if these men were prepared to back him, they must have confidence that he would succeed, so after his time at University and with the Forestry Commission in 1950 he made his way to London.

Chapter 4

With Alec Gibson
at College in London
and onto Opera

At the Royal Music College and Beyond

Kenneth enjoyed studying at the RMC in London. It was very different from the course in Forestry in Aberdeen. He was stimulated by his contacts and associations with Alexander Gibson, David Ward, Joan Sutherland and Julian Bream, all of whom had exceptional talent.

Being at the College gave him access to concerts at the Albert Hall with the best Artists. He with other students were able to go to Covent Gardens and Sadlers Wells to listen to rehearsals for free and spend all day there.

Kenneth auditioned for the Carl Rosa Opera Company where he expected to become a member of the chorus. The audition involved him singing 'The Flower Song' from Carmen. He was offered a contract as a principal Tenor at £15 per week, but he had to pay for his own accommodation out of this. The Principal had left to join Sadlers Wells and Carl Rosa offered Kenneth a Principal's contract in the 'Barber of Seville'

In 1953 he married Hedy Christine Matisse from Switzerland whom he met while in London. However because of his heavy commitments at that time, the honeymoon did not take place until 1955 when they visited Hedy's family in Switzerland.

Fellow Students at the RMC

Among those who were at the RMC at the same time
were
Alexander Gibson , later Sir Alexander Gibson who
studied piano. He became a leading British Conductor,
he was a fellow Scot who in 1959 returned to Scotland
as Principal Conductor of the Scottish National
Orchestra. While back home he founded Scottish
Opera.

David Ward was again a fellow Scot who after his
studies joined the chorus at Sadlers Wells Opera as a
Baritone.

Joan Sutherland was born in Sydney, Australia. She
had an international career as a Soprano as a result of
embarking on a series of concerts at the world's leading
opera houses. She was awarded Dame of the British
Empire in 1979.

Julian Bream was born in London. On his eleventh
birthday he was given a guitar and became somewhat of
a child protégé. At the age of twelve he won a Junior
Exhibition Award for his piano playing. This enabled
him to go to the RMC to study piano and cello.

A Singer not an Actor

When Hedy first met Kenneth she thought he was an actor, as he had been performing as an actor at College. He was performing in a play by Sheridan in which he played the part with a George Sanders accent. She was surprised when she first heard him sing which was towards the end of his fourth and final year at the RMC.

Principal Tenor

Being a Principal Tenor allowed him to afford to buy a car and to get married. However he felt uneasy about appearing in Opera, disliking the costumes and preferring to sing in English. Kenneth compared Opera to riding on a tramcar, going on the same lines all the time. Alexander Gibson, when Kenneth said he felt that Opera was boring replied that he must be with the wrong Opera company.

He had a bust up with the management of the Opera Company. Others had left the Company and Kenneth was asked to take the lead in two different Operas. The Company refused to offer an increase in salary to match Kenneth's new responsibilities. He handed in his notice an left the Company two weeks later when the tour at Stratford on Avon was completed

Leaving Opera

The fact that Kenneth wasn't happy and comfortable in Opera was a great loss to Opera as he had the potential to become a great British Opera star. He realised what was good about the Opera was that there was a repetition of performance, the same works over and over again, which eventually gets into the singer's voice. As a Tenor the voice lies in the top register to sing. Scottish songs and other materials which were not Opera required a much greater range to perform.

Yodelling

When they finally got to honeymoon Kenneth and Hedy holidayed in Switzerland with her family. He got to know his brother-in-law, who was the secretary of the William Tell Yodelling Choir, the official choir of Swiss railways. On one evening during their visit Kenneth was invited to join his brother-in-law as the choir had a rehearsal evening. He was fascinated that the rehearsal took place in the corner of a town centre restaurant, which was busy with locals and tourists both enjoying a meal and the rehearsal. The idea he felt he could emulate some time in the future in Scotland.

Chapter 5

The Decca Years

1955 to 1980

George Martin

Prior to an operation on his tonsils, Kenneth recorded five songs in 1950. One of the reasons he made the recordings was he wasn't sure what ability he would have to sing after the operation, so he would have evidence of his talents. The recordings were made available to Parlophone and came into the hands of George Martin who was with Parlophone at this time. George had known Kenneth from his student days in Aberdeen when George played the oboe in the University Orchestra.

When Kenneth and George met in London, George recalled that Kenneth had sung at his wedding. The wedding had taken place at Aberdeen University where George's first wife Sheena was a Principal Soprano.

George recognised Kenneth's talents and despite the fact that he was still a young man and George persuaded him to sign for Decca, the record company George had moved to from Parlophone. George wanted to let Kenneth see that there was a market for Scottish songs.
It was a road that Kenneth followed with great success. George Martin's career was to lead him to world wide fame and a knighthood, as he produce the 'Beatles' records.

Recording at Paisley Abbey

Decca, the recording company which Kenneth had a contract with, decided to make recordings at Paisley Abbey with probably the best choir in Scotland at that time. The album was to feature Sacred Songs and George McPhee, the organist at the Abbey made the arrangements for the recordings. The noise of the traffic, on the cobbled streets surrounding the Abbey made it very difficult to produce a recording to the standard the Decca required.

Decca asked the local Council if it were possible to divert the traffic, but the request was turned down. Kenneth had sung with the Paisley Police Choir, so he knew a number of the officers in charge of the Police Force in Paisley, when the Renfrew and Bute constabulary were asked to divert the traffic they were happy to do so at night.

The recording work took place over three session, from midnight to 3.00am, and besides the Abbey Choir there was a choir of 30 school boys. Because they were up to 3.00am to record, they were given the next morning off lessons. It was noted that these choir boys were usually the liveliest at 3.00am.

George McPhee

George McPhee, the organist at the Paisley Abbey who later became Professor George McPhee, got to know Kenneth in 1967 when Decca made an album of Sacred songs at the Abbey. He observed that Kenneth was not a great church goer, but brought a spiritual dimension to everything he did and was able to get inside the meaning of religious songs.

Kenneth, he observed was an all round musician who was a composer, and wrote two anthems, one of which was performed at his memorial service in 2010. He was both an arranger and conductor and on one occasion he both sang and conducted the orchestra.

Paisley Abbey

Paisley Abbey was founded in 1163 as a monastery if the Cluniac Order. The Abbey was founded by Walter Fitzalan. He was the first hereditary High Steward of Scotland and a forebear of the Royal House of Stewart, from which Queen Elizabeth 11 is descended. Worship at the Abbey has been offered for more than 800 years.

Duncan Creighton

Peter Ustinov visited the remote Fijian island of Levuka to find the legendary Duncan Creighton reputed to be a semi-recluse. He still wore a kilt and taught the native teenagers the dances of his own country.

While visiting with Duncan, Peter Ustinov had the opportunity to browse through his collection of carefully preserved vinyls. All the vinyls were by Kenneth McKellar and Ustinov was amazed that he hadn't appreciated how popular McKellar was amongst Scots and ex-pat Scots and in fact he had given a 'living legacy of music to the world'.
Source Booklet with CD Kenneth McKellar the Decca Years 1955 - 1975 Notes by Raymond Horricks

The Decca Years

Throughout the 1960s Kenneth was recording two albums a year for Decca. He made a recording of Handel's Arias with the conductor Sir Adrian Boult. Boult conducted the London Symphony Orchestra and he made the statement that "McKellar's recordings of Handel's Arias made him the foremost Handelian Tenor of his generation."

Kenneth made a recording of 'Kismet' with Adele Leigh, and fellow Scot Ian Wallace. He was especially praised for his album in 1961 'Songs of the Hebrides' which illustrated his desire to sing traditional songs from around the British Isles.

Included in aspects of his vast and growing repertoire, Kenneth made a tribute album to the Irish Tenor John McCormack and to his own relative Willie McCulloch.

Songs of the Hebrides

For this album Bob Sharples had put together a small ensemble. Kenneth chose the songs and introduced them to Bob who had not known of these Hebridean songs before. Marjorie Kennedy Fraser's arrangements were to be used with an ensemble providing a lightness of touch to each song. It was decided that Kenneth would provide and perform speaking links for each song. He spent the evening before each song was recorded in his hotel in Halfmoon St., in London writing the speaking links. Before each track Kenneth was heard walking on shingle. The recording of walking on the shingle was made in Hasting, so the noise was not provide by the shingle on Scottish beaches.

The Songs of Robert Burns

In all Decca made over forty albums with Kenneth including two highly acclaimed recordings, 'A Tribute to Robert Burns' in 1959 and 'Songs of Robert Burns' in 1960. When he recorded the Album 'The Songs of Robert Burns' the arrangements by Bob Sharples were unlike those on the Hebrides album. Burns songs are difficult to sing due to the range, as the tunes have been derived from fiddle tunes which have got a range which is challenging for the human voice to cope with.

The Arrangers

Bob Sharples was the main arranger for Kenneth for many years. He was born in Lancashire and spent time in the army rising to become a major and advancing his musical skills. He was the avuncular musical director of 'Opportunity Knocks', the talent show which featured Hughie Green. Kenneth's most requested recording was 'My Love is Like a Red, Red Rose' which he recorded with Decca in 1955 and he later recorded a stereo version in 1959. Bob was the arranger for which he was given a 'Best Arrangement Award' in the USA by Music America .

Another arranger who worked with Kenneth was Peter Knight who did the arrangement for 'Ae Fond Kiss' which he sang with the Irish singer Patricia Cahill. Peter Knight specialised in lush orchestrations.

The Great Duets

The great duets were recorded live at the Wigmore hall in London with Kenneth and Patricia Cahill. From the age of ten the Dublin born singer Patricia became known as the 'Irish Nightingale'. Her beautiful voice has a special 'something' which crosses all musical barriers. She recalls the experience of recording the Great Duets.
"Kenneth was a tenor I always admired. I loved his voice, a voice which was full of music. Imagine my

surprise when he asked me to make an album of duets. We met in London and discussed the songs and decided to put in two songs from our own countries. We recorded the album with a full orchestra conducted by Max Harris, a well know conductor and composer. We recorded the albums in three days meeting up to go through the harmonies of the songs to be recorded that day. All the songs were recorded from top to tail (from beginning to end) without any breaks. A little editing was done before the album was released. We listened and looked at each other and seemed to feel when to take a breath and finished notes together. We had never sung together before and I have to say that this album is one of my favourites. Kenneth was a lovely man, a true professional, with a lovely voice, and an absolute pleasure to work and sing with."

The Songs on the Album were : -
1. We Kiss in a Shadow
2. This is my Lovely Day
3. Ae Fond Kiss
4. Whispering Hope
5. I will walk with My Love
6. One Alone
7. One Hand, One Heart
8. My Dearest Dear
9. The Lark in the Clear Air
10. When the Children are Asleep
11. The Crooked Bawbee
12. Love's Old Sweet Song

Dame Vera Lynn

Kenneth never sang with Vera Lynn, but did stand hand in hand with her during a Royal Command Performance. It was decided by Decca to release an extended play record of Nursery Rhymes with the British Museum supplying the authentic words for each song.   Kenneth and Vera both recorded songs and the recordings were put together to form an extended play record. His songs included such nursery rhymes as 'Polly put the Kettle On' and 'Hey Diddle the Cat and the Fiddle' with Bob Sharples providing the accompaniments. Vera sang 'Girls and Boys come out to Play' and 'Sing a Song of Sixpence'. The venture proved to be very successful for Vera , Kenneth and Decca.

Some Highlights and Comments of Kenneth's recordings for Decca

1.   'Roamin' in the Gloamin'
   - sung with verve and panache
2.   'Skye Boat Song'
   - sounds as if it were composed by Bizet for conclusion in his Opera the 'Fair Maid of Perth.
3.   'Kalinka'
   - This popular chart item showed he could turn his hand to any song
4.   'The Longest Day'
   - From the film and sung inspiringly.

5.   'Maria'
     - by Leonard Bernstein from West Side Story.

It is acknowledged that the recording by Kenneth
     is the best by a Lyric Tenor.

6.   'She Moved Thru' the Fair'
     - at this recording Kenneth struck one note on the
     piano for a key and sung it through in just one
     take.

7.   'The De'il's Awa Wi' the Exciseman
     - Burns songs are as difficult to sing as any operatic
     aria, but Kenneth copes admirably with these
     songs, and in fact his recordings were considered
     by many to be the finest interpretations of Burns
     Songs.

8.   'To People Who Have Gardens'
     - The phrasing is always coherent and the words
     follow exactly on the rhythmic stress.

9.   'The Noon in the Deep Blue Sky'
     - This is from the Kennedy-Fraser collection and
     demonstrates how Kenneth was able 'To get inside'
     the composer's intention.

10. 'Great is Jehovah'
     -Although this is sacred music it makes operatic
     demands on a tenor's voice.

11. 'God be in my Head'
     - By Bach, He was backed by just ten voices from
     the Paisley Abbey and the organist George
     McPhee, and includes special harmonic changes.

12. 'Ae Fond Kiss'
    - this is a duet with Patricia Cahill and is a wonderful version of this Burns song.
13. 'This is my Lovely Day'
    - Part of the great duets where Kenneth and Patricia were showboating with this song.

The source for these comments was a booklet entitled, 'Kenneth McKellar the Decca years' a 2 CD set of varied musical accomplishments of Scotland's finest tenor .

The Decca years were good for both Kenneth and Decca. The albums which were issued brought Kenneth's talents to a world wide audience and for Decca a financially successful venture.

<u>Top Tenor dumped by Decca</u>

The following article appeared on Wednesday 30th September 1987 in the Evening Times.
'Kenneth McKellar's years at Decca started when he signed for them in 1955. When Decca was taken over by Polygram at the beginning of the 1980's, a decision was made to release artists not making a fast enough buck, and they would be dropped from the company's roster.

After recording over forty albums for Decca Kenneth had been turned out and his albums consigned to the ranks of the back catalogue bin. McKellar stated " I am

not the least bit upset as my contract had run out."
He was then pestered by a local record company
Lismore to sign for them and has become their biggest
selling artist. A new album , a collection of Burns songs
accompanied by the Edinburgh quartet will be released
at Christmas 1987.'

Chapter 6

As 'Jamie' at the Alhambra, Glasgow

The Glasgow Alhambra

The Alhambra was Glasgow's favourite revue and pantomime showcase. The theatre opened six days before Christmas in 1910 and was often referred to as the rich man's Glasgow Music Hall. It opened as a Variety Theatre 'with a difference', as the other theatres in Glasgow were all running shows twice a night. The Alhambra set out to operate only once- nightly at 7.30pm.

Glasgow was proud of its new theatre with posters proclaiming 'An Unparalleled Programme'. The Glasgow audiences had accepted that the Alhambra was the kind of theatre they had wanted for many years.

Dick Hurran, the producer has made world wide talent-spotting visits. As a result of these visits, speciality and musical acts from the USA were booked for regular appearances at the theatre.

The Five - Past Eight Show in 1959 was described 'As Scotland's successful revue since the war'. Four hundred and fifty thousand were attracted to the show which was one in ten of the population in Scotland.

Many of the great names of the British music hall and of dramatic theatre performed at the Alhambra. Among those were Lily Langtry (The Jersey Lily),

Anna Neagle, starred with Jack Buchanan in a show 'Stand up and sing'. In 1925 a most exciting and glamorous evening took place when the show 'No, No,Nanette' was staged with special numbers , like 'Tea for Two' and 'I want to be Happy'.

As time moved on Pantomime sessions starring Jimmy Logan, who made his panto debut at the Alhambra, along with Stanley Baxter, Rikki Fulton, David Hughes and Kenneth McKellar replaced the Variety Shows.

The Theatre then switched to having a Revue at Christmas time which led to the final glitter at the Alhambra's thousand and one glamorous nights.

Many wept at the passing of the Alhambra which went out of the theatre -goers lives after sixty years. Those who had the opportunity to visit this theatre and its great shows have been left with wonderful and lasting memories.

Rikki Fulton

In his book 'Is it that time already?' Rikki Fulton wrote of his feeling on the demise of the Alhambra.
" The Alhambra theatre in Wellington St., with its two thousand seven hundred and fifty seats, became the home of the famous Five-Past Eight Show and was in my opinion perhaps the best theatre in Europe. After the death of Stewart Cruikshank, Peter Donald took the

reins and within a short time Howard and Wyndham , the owners of the theatre had got rid of most of their theatre properties. They offered the Alhambra to the Glasgow Corporation along with the'King's Theatre in Bath Street. The King's was sold to Glasgow Corporation in 1966, but the Alhambra offered in 1969 was refused because of the outlay required for purchase and the cost of the upkeep of two theatres. Peter Donald's threat of demolition was carried out in 1971.

A Wish for Jamie

Stewart Cruikshank Jnr. who was the managing director for the Howard and Wyndham Theatres, had an ambition to have a big all Scottish pantomime with magical Christmas stories in fantasy and music. It would have a Scot called Jamie as its' hero. He wanted to produce a show which got away from the 'Cinderella' and 'Jack in the Beanstalk' kind of pantomimes.

The person to produce the first 'Jamie' pantomime, 'A Wish for Jamie' was a dapper little Australian, Freddie Carpenter. Freddie said he was shocked to learn that Scotland had no established fairy tales of its own, with her proud history, traditions and clans. Germany had Grimm's Fairy Tales, Denmark had Hans Christian Anderson and England had Dick Whittington and his Cat. Freddie felt the new pantomime would make history, by giving Scotland a panto fairy tale of her own.

Stewart Cruikshank's Comments

In a programme note Stewart Cruikshank wrote "Jamie has now established himself as a prime favourite in the annals of pantomime. I don't think it is exaggerating that the combination of Jamie, Kenneth McKellar , Rikki Fulton and producer Freddie Carpenter is without doubt is one of the most successful stage teams of all times". Kenneth McKellar said " 'Jamie' is not a pantomime, but more of a musical, a Scottish Brigadoon. These Christmas seasons were the happiest I had ever done. Whether it was the joy of the character I was playing or the other characters I was playing with, I really don't know."

For Rikki Fulton, Kenneth praised his work as a versatile dame. In the Jamie shows Rikki took various guises, farm owner, highland dancer, jolly hockey stick schoolgirl, a beatnik and a bluebell dancing girl. He was screamingly funny in each role.

The Cast of Jamie

The first Jamie Panto was staged at the Alhambra, Glasgow on a December evening in 1960. The star was the singer Kenneth McKellar creating the role of the hero Jamie,and with him were Rikki Fulton as the gorgeously gowned dame and Reg Varney as Percy the young English Farmhand. Fay Lenore, a personality girl originally from Tyneside who had featured with

Norman Wisdom at the London Palladium,was the dashing Principal Boy Donald, brother of Jamie.

Fay's own life story was equally romantic. She had married at the close of a previous Alhambra pantomime Mother Goose, and had settled down as the wife of a young Loch Lomondside farmer and Highland Games Championship Jay Scott. Her home at the time of Jamie was the island of Inchmurrin in the middle of Loch Lomond. Reg Varney, a Londoner from Enfield had still to make a national name through the television series 'On the Buses'. He had already played a most likeable 'Buttons' in a Cinderella Pantomime at the Alhambra in Glasgow, five years before, and he knew the warmth of a Glasgow audience.

The part of 'Fergus' the Laird's son and of King Frog were 'doubled' by a Scots actor Russell Hunter. He had returned to his native Clydeside from an acting job in England. Little did Hunter realise at that time that ten years later he would become a star name thanks to being featured in a television series known nationally as 'Callam'. John Law a young Glasgow man who had once been a telephone copy taker on a Scottish morning newspaper and had then moved south to London to write scripts. He had written the book 'A Wish for Jamie' as well as some of the music and lyrics. The settings and costumes were by the ace London designer Berkeley Sutcliffe, and the choreography was by Peter Darrell. The Western Theatre Ballet and the George

Mitchell Singers, also adorned the cast list.

Source List 'The Good Auld Days' by Gordon Irving published by Jupiter Books (London Ltd.)

The 1963 Pantomime

With his usual ability to do something different , Freddie Carpenter decided for the 1963 Pantomime to use a ventriloquist dummy as a major character in the 'Jamie Show'. 'Lenny the Lion' was partnered by ventriloquist Terry Hall . This was the first time a 'dummy' had been used in a pantomime plot. Freddie's gamble paid off and the audiences both adults and children really took to the lovable Lenny.

Lenny was introduced to the world in 1954 at a summer season in Blackpool. He had since then built up a great following with a fan club numbering over 25,000. Terry Hall was born in Oldham in Lancashire and he took up ventriloquism when he was just 15 years of age.

Pantomime was a Smash Hit

The Evening Times under the heading 'Panto was a Smash' reported the following

'Kenneth McKellar will go down in the history books for his role in A Wish for Jamie. Scotland's very first original panto.

It opened at the Alhambra Theatre in 1960, against the wishes of the directors who openly wept when they saw the final dress rehearsal. They were convinced they had a massive flop on their hands. But they were wrong.

"The opening night was like nothing you'll ever see in Glasgow again". said McKellar, who played the lead role of Jamie, a love-struck villager besotted by a beautiful girl. " The audience just loved it."

Jamie was a smash. It ran for two seasons, a sequel ran for another season and part three followed the next year.

"And do you know what the really sad thing is?" asked the show's former principal.

"The theatre where all those thousands of people laughed and cried with Jamie, doesn't even exist any more."

Programme notes on Kenneth Mc Kellar in the third year of 'Jamie in 1962.

" I remember Freddy Carpenter told me he was having a pantomime around and for me, I was very flattered." stated Kenneth McKellar " I couldn't visualise what it really meant." It meant that Kenneth Scotland's biggest box office attraction is now playing Jamie for the third year . His views on Jamie are interesting, "Although it is patently a pantomime." Kenneth stated and he went on to say "It has never appeared quite that way to me," This was Kenneth's seventh panto for Howard and Wyndham and he spent a Christmas season at the Kings, Glasgow in 'Old Chelsea' Kenneth said "That whatever I do in future I want to work with Freddie Carpenter, he's quite fantastic."

Programme notes on Kenneth Mc Kellar in the fourth year of 'Jamie in 1963.

Jamie for the fourth season running, Kenneth McKellar had created a new hero in the repertoire of pantomime. A hero written especially for him, and the pantomime written round him. That's how highly Stewart Cruikshank and Freddie Carpenter rate our most popular Scottish singer . It isn't by any means of course Kenneth's only medium. Each year sees him branching out further afield.

He has now gone full circle in the theatre where he started by singing Opera leads with the Carl Rosa company. Last Autumn he fulfilled another ambition when he sang Macheath in the 'Beggars Opera' in Paris and on BBC TV. And before that, during the summer he staged his own show for the first time in this country, A Touch of Tartan which had packed out performances in Aberdeen and Edinburgh.

Since last year's 'Jamie' he has sung at the Edinburgh Festival and completed a successful BBC TV series from

London. His output of records is still unflagging all over the world. Only Mantovani sells more records for the Decca Company that Kenneth. His latest which he considers his best is an album of 'Favourite Songs and Ballads'. and two Extended Play records for children entitled 'Nursery Rhymes' which contains fifty titles and was recorded in conjunction with Vera Lynn.

Photographs

The Photographs included in this book have been available courtesy of the following.

Photograph	Courtesy of
Front Cover of Kenneth	Paisley Reference Library
1. Mary Street Paisley	Cath Cameron
2. Baronscourt Gardens	Cath Cameron
3. John Neilston School	Cath Cameron
4. Paisley Abbey	Cath Cameron
5. Dunoon Pier	Cath Cameron
6. Inellan Bowling Green	Cath Cameron
7. Queens Hall Dunoon	Cath Cameron
8. Toward Point	Cath Cameron
9. View from holiday home on Seil Island	Cath Cameron
10. Corran Halls Oban	Cath Cameron
11. Bridge to Seil Island	G. Brummer
12. Kenneth on bike	Paisley Reference Library
13. McKellar's Shop	Paisley Museum
14. Primary 2 Class	Peter Stewart
15. Panto at Alhambra	Mitchell Library
16. Kenneth in full Highland dress	Mitchell Library
17. Alhambra Foursome	Mitchell Library
18. Kenneth the Decca Years	Paisley Reference Library
19. The Alhambra Glasgow	Mitchell Library
Back Cover Top Looking to the South	Dane Clark
Back Cover Bottom Looking North	Dane Clark

The Tenement building at 12, Mary Street, Paisley, where Kenneth McKellar was born.

The McKellars moved to 6, Barons Court Gardens. Paisley, nearly out in the country.

The main building at the John Neilston School with the distinctive Porridge Bowl.

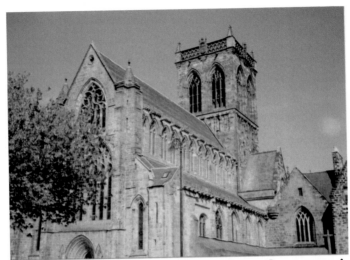

The impressive Paisley Abbey, where the memorial service for Kenneth took place.

Dunoon pier, a view from the Calmac Ferry arriving at the pier. From 30th Jun 2011 the Ferry took passengers only .

The Inellan bowling green where Kenneth, his brothers and Dad spent summer holiday evenings.

The Queens Hall Dunoon where Kenneth performed in summer shows.

The Mckellar's fished for mackerel off Toward Point, near Dunoon.

A beautiful view from Kenneth and Hedy's holiday home on Seil Island near Oban.

The Corran Halls in Oban.
Kenneth performed many summer seasons here.

The Bridge across the Atlantic to Seil Island where the
McKellars had their holiday home.

Kenneth Living life in the fast lane.

Referred to by the locals as McKellar's Wine shop, at the corner of Causeyside St., and Canal St, Paisley.

The Primary Two class at the John Neilston school in Paisley in 1933. From left to right 1. Douglas Lamond, 3. Iain McPherson, 8. Peter D. Stewart 10. Kenneth McKellar, in kilt 11. Jim Mormond.

Pantomime at the Alhambra with Lennie the Lion, Terry Hall, Kenneth McKellar and Rikki Fulton.

Kenneth in full Highland dress ready to entertain.

An Alhambra foursome of Reg Varney, Rikki Fulton, Faye Lenore and Kenneth McKellar

Kenneth during the Decca years

The Alhambra Theatre Glasgow

Chapter   7

'The West Sound
Burns Suppers'

Thomas Sutherland

Thomas Sutherland was born in Falkirk, Scotland on the 3rd May 1931.   He obtained a BSc in Agriculture from Glasgow University   in the 1950s. He moved to the United States and gained a Masters degree and a Doctorate   in animal breeding from Iowa State University .   He then taught Animal Sciences at Colorado State University for 26 years.

Tom moved to Beirut University and in June 1985, he, returned from holiday in Colorado, and was kidnapped by members of Islamic Jihad whilst in a the limousine normally used by the President of the University, Calvin Plimpton.   This may have been an incidence of mistaken identity.

When John McCarthy, an English born hostage was released in August, 1991, he was able to tell Tom's wife Jean, that Tom had spasmodic use of a battery radio which gave him great comfort, the BBC World Service being his favourite station.   On the 25th January each year, the date of Robert Burns' birth Jean sent   a red rose   of love to Tom's captors in the hope that it would reach him. When she learned that Tom had access to a radio now and again   she thumbed through their record collection and came across the Burn's Song sung by Kenneth McKellar who had always been Tom's favourite singer. Jean asked the BBC World Service if they would play it and miraculously Tom heard the recording.   On his release from captivity in November

1991, Tom at a Press conference, declared that when he heard the song it was the only time he had wept throughout his ordeal.

Press Conference

A Press conference was held in the American Military Hospital in Wiesbaden, Germany, and watching it on a BBC TV News channel in Scotland was Joe Campbell, Managing Director of West Sound Radio in Ayr. In those days West Sound hosted one the largest and most prestigious Burns Suppers in the world and was due to hold its next one a few weeks after Tom's release. Singing the songs of Burns as only he could, would be Kenneth McKellar. Joe contacted Tom by fax in Germany and the invitation to Tom and Jean to be special guests at the West Sound Burns Supper in Glasgow, where Tom would meet his hero, Kenneth McKellar, was immediately accepted!

The day arrived and as usual on these occasions the artistes met in the afternoon to rehearse with the orchestra or band and it was in the afternoon that Kenneth and Tom first met. Ken explained that he couldn't possibly sing "O My Love is Like Red, Red Rose" for very good reason. His wife, Hedy, had died suddenly only a year or so before and it had been her favourite song. Ken felt the emotion of singing it would be too much for him, and Tom understood perfectly. The evening came and 1100 men and women listened spellbound to Scotland's greatest singer as he sang three Burns songs. Then he stepped up to the microphone and said: "There is a song that is very dear to me. I know that it's dear to Tom Sutherland, and for him I will try to sing it." There wasn't a dry eye in the house and Jack Webster of the Herald newspaper was later to write that the occasion was the most emotional he had witnessed.

A Holiday Cottage

Ken and Hedy adored the west coast of Scotland and bought a holiday cottage on the Island of Seil, seven miles south-west of Oban. The Clachan Bridge which linked the island to the mainland was designed in 1792 by Thomas Telford and became known as "the bridge over the Atlantic."

Frances Shand Kydd

When Hedy died Ken decided to sell the cottage and it was bought by Mrs Frances Shand Kydd, the mother of Diana, Princess of Wales. She owned Ardencaple Estate on the island and decided to downsize. She was living at the cottage when she received news of Diana's tragic death. She and Ken were close friends and Joe Campbell recalls seeing a photograph of Diana aged 7 or 8 sitting on Ken's grand piano dangling her long legs as she listened to him playing and singing to her.

The Burns Suppers

Frances spoke at one of West Sound's Burns Suppers where she told the huge audience that she ran a newsagent's shop in Oban! She was precisely the sort of person Kenneth liked. Unpretentious and with a great sense of humour. On that occasion she celebrated her 57th birthday with 1100 people and during the evening "daughter number three" as she referred to Diana, rang her to wish her a happy birthday.

Joe Campbell, who organised and chaired these Burns Suppers, believes that although there were many marvellous speakers and singers featured over the years, such as Edward Heath, Donald Dewar, Malcolm Rifkind, George Younger, David Owen, John Smith, Sir Clement Freud, etc., Kenneth was always the star attraction, not only to the huge audience but to his fellow performers.

Each year the Burns Suppers were held on a Saturday evening in January. At 2.00pm in the afternoon of these days a bandcall was held for the speakers/artistes to test the microphones and go over their items.   On the Thursday before the event, Jane McKellar, Ken's only daughter, called Joe Campbell from Sydney to tell him she was making a surprise visit to Glasgow without her Dad knowing she was coming, and wondered if she could get a ticket for the Burns Supper. They hatched a plot.   She would be Joe's guest, and a room was booked for her on the Friday evening at the hotel in which the Burns Supper would be held.

Ken's pianist was Walter Blair, a brilliant accompanist on many of his recordings, and capable of playing Ken's arrangements for Burns songs which although beautiful, were complicated and required much rehearsing. At 2.00pm   on the dot on the Saturday, Ken arrived for the bandcall to be met with the news outside the huge ballroom that Walter had called off sick but that a young female pianist had been hired. He nearly turned on his heels to walk out declaring that the arrangements were extremely difficult, but „Joe persuaded him to meet the girl anyway. He walked into the ballroom and up to the piano where "the girl" was sitting with her back to him. When she turned round, the great singer cursed in Anglo Saxon language, but after embracing his daughter and with tears streaming down his face, he said to Joe, "you're forgiven!"

Chapter 8

An Ambassador
for Song and Entertainment

The Songwriter

Kenneth stated "I always had a song going on in my head, particularly when I was working on stage. The producers of a 'Wish for Jamie' indicated they needed a couple of new songs, so I wrote the ballad 'The Tartan'." 'The Tartan' has been covered by some forty artists, he also wrote 'The Royal Mile' which was heard by more than 4 million people during the televised opening of the 1986 Commonwealth Games in Edinburgh. He also turned his hand to writing comedy songs and two in particular are 'The Pan Drap' song and 'The Midges' both of which have passed with tongue in cheek into Scottish folklore.

The words of these songs are included below .

The Midges

The Lord put the Garden of Eden on earth,
and it's north of the Tweed believe,
Aye, Scotland's the place and the whole human race,
Started with MacAdam and Eve.

Chorus
The midges, the midges, I'm no gonnae kid ye's
The midges are really the limit,
Wi' teeth like piranhas, they drive ye bananas
If ye let them get under yer simmit!

In six days or under, he finished his wonder,
Except for the Forth and Tay bridges,
Then always a bloke for a practical joke
He made Scotland the home of the midges

Back in 1314, proud Edward was keen,
To take Scotland into his care,
But he made a U-turn when he reached Bannockburn,
Just a few weeks before the Glasgow Fair.

The midges let loose by King Robert the Bruce,
Straight into the English they tore,
So they ran off in tears and for six hundred   long years,
They've been blocking the A74!

Now never forget, when the sun's going to set,
And the midges arise on Loch Eck,
Like vampires you see , played by Christopher Lee,
They'll give you a pain in the neck!

You can smack them and whack them; in vain you'll
attack them,
They know every move that you make,
If you manage to kill yin, another half million,
Are ready to come tae the wake!

Now Torquil the piper's a giant of a man,
With a sporran as long as your arm,
And in Oban he's known, for the sounds of his drone,
And a pibroch of real highland charm!

But they're sighing and sobbing the ladies of Oban,
Torquil is not what he was,
Since a midge in Glenbranter, got hold of   his chanter,
And carried it off in its jaws.

As recorded by Kenneth McKellar date not given
Tune similar to Matt McGinn's   "Red Yo-yo".

The Pan Drap song

Verse   1

My Granny has a sweet tooth,
The only one she's got,
A monument to local sweetie shops,
Altho' her life was dreary ,
She managed to be cheery,
After sixty years O' suckin' lemon drops,
She favoured Dolly Mixtures,
For an evening at the pictures,
I know for sometimes she took me along
I would sit upon her lap,
And share her sugar -ally strap
And going home she would sing this song.

Chorus
Give me a Pan-drap, a Pan-drap,
The thing what has made me, what I am today,
Its strong, Its white it tastes just right,
And chases all the nasty smells away

I need a Pan-drap, a Pan-drap,
I need it now and I will tell you why,
Besides my Adam's apple, a pan drop down my thrapple,
Will always put a twinkle in my eye

Verse 2
When she was eighty-three
She got the MBE,
For her services to the sweetie trade,
The only ones who knocked her ,
Were her dentist and her doctor,
She's a bad example , so they say.
But she was proud like Alice,
To be summoned to the Palace,
The family shed a patriotic tear,
When her Majesty bent down,
Said to Philip "Hold my Crown"
and whispered in Granny's ear

Chorus
Repeated

Turning his hand to comedy

Monty Python came to Kenneth's attention when he was performing at Blackpool. He decided to write a sketch for Monty Python for some future show. The sketch was entitled 'The Secret Policeman's Ball' and he sent the script to Ian McNaughton who was the producer of the Monty Python shows. Ian responded positively and asked if Kenneth would be prepared to appear in the sketch. Kenneth declined , the sketch went ahead and was a great success.

Kenneth was slightly coy about his sketch for Monty Python, saying "I just dashed of something at the time, I never ever met John Cleese, or any of the other members of the team, although John Cleese did write two very nice letters and mentioned me in his auto-biography. I had scripted all my own radio and television series so I was experienced in writing. Although it was exciting to write for Monty Python I didn't see a new career opportunity."

Ian McNaughton   1925 - 2002

Ian was originally an actor who went on to become a television producer and director. He was born and brought up in Glasgow. He produced Spike Milligan's programme 'Q' which was a big influence on the Monty Python team. In a television tribute to Spike Milligan screened in 2011 Terry Jones, had indicated that the

Python team had stolen McNaughton from the 'Q' programme.   Ian was both the director and producer who got 'Monty Python's Circus' flying.

Johnny Beattie

The Monty Python writing wasn't Kenneth's first venture into comedy writing.   Kenneth had appeared with Johnny Beattie, the comedian who later became a member of the cast of the BBC Scotland's soap 'River City'.   They had appeared together in various shows and while in Aberdeen for a ten week summer season, Johnny and Ken did a comedy double act.   At the change of programme they used to go Herd's café opposite the theatre to write new material.   Johnny recalls the fun they had in writing the material and how well their material was received, with surprise by the audience who had expected to hear Kenneth sing but not to be part of a comedy act.

Dickie Henderson   1922 - 1985

Kenneth   also wrote material for the comedian Dickie Henderson who had compered Sunday Night at the London Palladium, and hosted a 120 episodes of the Dickie Henderson Show, and Kenneth was in partnership in producing comedy sketches with Bob Monkhouse.

The Romantic Scotland of Kenneth McKellar

Besides comedy and song writing, Kenneth had success in other areas of writing, as well as writing and producing a book 'The Romantic Scotland of Kenneth McKellar' in picture and song, which is now in its third edition.

According to his mother the first word that Kenneth spoke was "Columba". He in fact was referring to the paddle steamer which daily sailed from Greenock to Ardrishaig on Loch Fyne. The Clyde and the islands on the Clyde became familiar to Kenneth and he came to realise that most of the places of interest in Scotland have a song written about them.

The Islands of the Hebrides have their own songs including songs for Skye, Uist, Lewis, Mull, Mingulay, Eriskay, Jura, Islay and Barra. Such songs as 'Loch Lomond', 'The Royal Mile', 'The Flowers of the Forest', and the 'Road to the Isles', all depict the romance and the glory of specific events and bring the very stuff of history to life.

The book contained
The words of forty songs Kenneth had helped to make famous.
Notes by Kenneth about the songs and the locations.
Stunning pictures in colour by Jarrold Colour.

The Eurovision   Song Contest

In 1966 the United Kingdom organisers were keen that the country should win the Eurovision contest, after several years when there had been near misses.
Kenneth was chosen to represent the United Kingdom. He was an unusual choice to participate in this light weight 'Pop' music contest. He wanted to appear in a suit but the organisers insisted he wear full Scottish dress, which he was unhappy about as many of the audience assumed that as he wore a kilt that he was representing Scotland.

The song Kenneth was asked to sing was a 'A Man without Love' by Peter Callander and   Cyril Ornadel. The song came ninth out of eighteen countries taking part, which was the United Kingdom's lowest position to that date, and it was only saved from ignominy by receiving top marks from a laughing Irish panel.

The record reached to number thirty in the charts, Peter Callander who wrote the lyrics stated after the contest. "The song didn't have a chance of reaching number one, McKellar shouldn't have worn the kilt.   If the song had been given to Tony Bennett   everyone would have said what a great song."

It is unlikely that 'A Man without Love'   would have beaten the winner Merci Cherie from Austria.
In 1967 the United Kingdom did win with the song

'Puppet on a String' sung by Sandie Shaw.   Kenneth didn't look back fondly on this experience.   He felt the approach Terry Wogan had when he was involved in the Eurovision, when he treated the whole contest very light heartedly, was the correct approach.   He felt that a number of those who attended the contest used the event as an opportunity for an expenses paid trip and there was no need for them to be there at all.

Kenneth McKellar 'A True Scot'

Despite his many overseas tours Kenneth's heart always lay in Scotland.   He had life membership of all the principle societies of Scottish origins throughout the world.

He became a trustee of the Scottish International Educational Trust which is an organisation set up to sponsor Scottish talent all over the world.   A fellow trustee was Sir Sean Connery who had been Kenneth's friend for more than forty years.

Sir Sean   stated of Kenneth "He worked tirelessly in the interests of artistic talent in Scotland using   his huge international profile to encourage young Scots to excel.   Kenneth's death is an enormous loss to the nation and above all to his family and friends to whom I send my condolences".

The Trust is funded by Sir Sean Connery and other celebrity members of the committee were Sir Jackie Stewart, Andy Irvine, and the late Sir Alexander Gibson. In 1990 nearly £60,000 was awarded to students based in Edinburgh.

The Trust was dear to Kenneth's heart and he stated "We would like to give more help. People come to us with projects that would be beneficial to Scotland or benefit individual Scots for something special."

Despite his busy life Kenneth sat on the board of directors of Radio Clyde, which at   one time was the most successful commercial radio station in Great Britain. On December 1st 1973, Radio Clyde began broadcasting to Glasgow and the West of Scotland. The first record played was 'The Song of the Clyde' sung by Kenneth.   The same recording was featured over the opening titles of the 1963 film 'Billy Liar' which starred Tom Courtenay as Billy and Julie Christie as Liz.   The film belonged to 'the kitchen sink drama movement' and in 2004 the magazine 'Total Film' named 'Billy Liar' the twelfth in their list of Greatest British films of all times.

<u>Vote No and No Again</u>

Kenneth held his own opinions on various issues and wasn't concerned whether these views were popular or not. During the debate on devolution McKellar surprised and angered many in Scotland when he wrote a newspaper article in August 1997.

The article was entitled 'Vote No and No Again ', where he expressed his opposition to any thoughts of a Scottish Parliament and to eventually Independence for Scotland.

On this matter he was very much a Unionist and expressed very definitely his views that Scotland should always remain part of the United Kingdom.   He felt no conflict of interest to these views and his lifetime efforts to promote all that was good about Scotland, throughout the world.

Overseas tours

1959
One cannot   underestimate the pleasure McKellar brought to thousands of expatriate Scots, and   in the process, he did much to publicise Scottish traditions and culture.   He achieved this without over-egging the tartan connection, rather, he was proud of his Scottish origins and loved the music.   It showed.   One of his first tours to the US in 1959 was with his friend the bandleader Jimmy Shand.   It was the first of numerous such tours the two made - especially to Australia and to New Zealand - and they all were a resounding success.
1960
He increased his profile around the world, beginning a series of North American tours in 1959, appearing   in concerts in Germany and France, touring South Africa and, 1960, setting off in the first of fifteen tours of

Australia and New Zealand with a company including the Scottish country dance, king -pin, accordionist Jimmy Shand and Alec Finlay, the comedian.

On a tour to South Africa Kenneth was joined by Moira Anderson and Chic Murray the comedian. Chic was excited and delighted to make the tour saying "Oh I love to go to Durban in a turban." Both Moira and Kenneth did their level best to support Chic who was now 'On his own', in that before this tour his wife Maidie, had decided not to go to South Africa.

While in South Africa Chic was invited to play a side-kick to Orson Wells in a new James Bond movie 'Casino Royal'. Initially Chic wasn't sure when he got the call whether it was Moira, who was known as a practical joker, winding the 'Big Man' up.

Besides touring South Africa, Kenneth visited Rhodesia, now Zimbabwe. While there he made recordings, took part in radio and television shows and undertook an extensive concert tour.

1991
In 1991 after his wife died Kenneth visited New Zealand again. On a visit to Dunedin, he was thrilled to meet up with the Australian baritone Peter Dawson, who was one of his favourite singers. On another occasion he concluded by singing 'My Love is Like a Red, Red Rose. After the concert a young couple made their way to talk

to him. They told him that they had planned to settle in New Zealand, but when they heard that Burns song it made them so home-sick they decided there and then to return home to Scotland.

He did much to popularise Scottish culture and traditions. He always wore the kilt with pride and as he toured America, Canada Australia and New Zealand regularly he brought misty eyed comfort to home-sick ex-pats.

A Special Welcome

Kenneth   loved visiting New Zealand maybe it was because the South or South Island was very like Scotland.   He was moved by the welcome he was given wherever he appeared , with capacity audiences of 3,000.   Buses were run from the centre of Dunedin for people to see his arrival at the airport and there were hundreds there to give him a   pop-star type reception. He was sure this sort of thing would not have happened in Scotland or for that matter anywhere through out the British Isles. During his visit to New Zealand he had taken part in a six concert tour.

While in New Zealand, one local critic wrote "Kenneth McKellar charmed and sang his way into the hearts of everybody in the theatre.   If a singer can reach his age and still give forth a pure controlled tone with clear diction and no loss of pitch, then Mr McKellar has managed to accomplish a great feat, and I would not doubt will be singing just as well ten years from now." In response to those comments Kenneth stated " I would like to have a contract to that effect.   It was a really wonderful experience and makes you wonder what you are doing wrong here in Scotland.   Maybe I have been around too long.   That kind of reaction gave me a fill-up, makes me feel that I am going to go on until people tell me to stop."

Information on Overseas Tours

It has proved difficult to obtain information on many of the overseas tours which Kenneth took part in.   This is why in this section of this chapter there are large gaps in the dates of the overseas tours which have been featured.   In the autobiographies and biographies of others who went on tour with Kenneth little or no detail is given of overseas tours.   We may need to wait until Moira Anderson   publishes her autobiography to gain more insight to the overseas tours of Kenneth and the others who toured with Moira.

Successful recordings

Kenneth's talents allowed him to record every type of Scottish Song along with operatic Arias.   His Handel's Arias were particularly loved and his recording of 'Where 'er you walk' became a perennial favourite of Radio 2's programme, 'Your Hundred Best Tunes'. His recordings of the lighter Verdi tenor roles were also much praised for their finesse and it was considered a shame that he restricted himself to so little operatic work in the theatre.

His album 'The World of Kenneth McKellar' issued in 1969 had ten weeks in the U.K. album charts. In 1970 Kenneth recorded an album 'Ecco Di Napoli' which contained Italian arias. The album was successful and spent ten weeks in the U.K. album charts. He was comfortable in singing in different languages and was able to use very authentic accents. His wife Hedy, was a fluent speaker in French, Spanish, English, German and Italian.

The Lismor years

After his contract with Decca had finished, Kenneth was persuaded to join Lismor Records which was based in Scotland. In 1983 and 1985, he added two Scottish recordings on the Lismor label to his catalogue featuring some of his own arrangements of songs old and new. The albums were entitled 'McKellar in Scotland' and 'Highland Journey'

In April 1991 a record was released in which he explored new territory. With only a piano accompaniment and mainly to his own arrangements he sang a mixture of twenty-two Welsh, Irish and Scottish songs, many of which he had never recorded before, under the overall title 'Land of My Heart's Desire' , one of the famous Hebridean melodies.These recording were made at the Cava studio off Sauchiehall Street. Being for voice and piano only the record allowed him full range, in interpretation of songs. He said "The reason for choosing that particular studio was that it had a cracking Bosendorfer piano. This is a German make and artists like Oscar Peterson won't play on anything else. It has a distinctive sound, particularly at the brass end....so sonorous (Having or producing a full, deep, or rich sound. ...). There were no special effects, when you sing with a piano only, there is nowhere to hide, you can't hide behind a lot of echo and noise and things like that, it's just you and the piano. You've just got to do it," he says.

Bob McDowell of Lismor   says "Recording 22 numbers was a mammoth task but Kenneth is such a professional, it went without a hitch". Accompanying him for the recording sessions was Walter Blair, professor of piano at the Royal Scottish Academy of Music and Drama. " If you build up a collection of good piano arrangements like this it will work very nicely,   as they can be used again out on tour and people will have heard the recording and recognise the arrangement". Previously, Kenneth had produced all the orchestrations for a record of Jacobite songs and also did the arrangements for all the instruments for the eighteen piece orchestra, for a second selection Jacobean songs which was recorded and released in 1991.

To keep the airways open he went through the scales every day of the year and sat and sang snatches of songs at the piano in his home.

Showstoppers

Joe Campbell hosted a Sunday evening programme on West Sound Radio called 'Showstoppers'. On one occasion Joe invited Kenneth to be his guest, not for the first time. Kenneth suggested that they would play and reflect on ten of his favourite recordings. The recordings he chose were:-
1. My song is all that I can bring to you.
2. Scotland the brave
3. My Love is like a Red, Red, Rose.
4. Kishmul's Galley
5. Come oe'r the Stream Charlie
6. Deidre's Farewell
7. Dido's Lament
8. Thanks to my Brethren- How Vain is Man?
9. Sound the Alarm
10 The Midges

These ten recordings showed the range of songs Kenneth was able to sing, from Burns and other Scottish songs, to items by Handel and his own composition, 'The Midges.'

A Popular Guest Artist

Kenneth received invitations to appear on various
Television shows including;
The Harry Secombe show
The Rolf Harris show
The Nana Mouskouri show
The Good Old Days

He always appeared in fine Highland dress and usually
sang songs from his Scottish song repertoire.   He
displayed   confidence in his performance and seemed
to enjoy the opportunities to display his talents to a
wider audience.   Kenneth and Harry Secombe were
great friends and had a deep appreciation for each
others musical abilities.

'Top of the Pops'
One of Kenneth McKellar's accomplishments was to
blaze a trail that led to classical stars such as Luciano
Pavarotti and Kiri Te Kanawa appearing on the BBC's
'Top of the Pops'

Kenneth embraced contemporary   popular music and
in 1966 he had a single in the top thirty, and was
instrumental in narrowing what was a gap between the
different kinds of music, from classical to pop.   He was
comfortable in recording such songs as 'Strangers in
Paradise', a much covered song that would be
considered to be from the pop music idiom.

This is your Life - Kenneth McKellar

On 2nd January,1991, his wife Hedy persuaded him to join her at a TV studio in London. To his surprise, he was greeted by the genial Michael Aspell, host of 'This is Your Life' show who with the assistance of the 'Big Red Book' took Kenneth through his lifetime of experiences. Those who allow themselves to participate in the show were referred to as 'victims'.

The stars who participated with Kenneth in the show included the Scottish soprano Moira Anderson, who had appeared with Kenneth in many shows both at home and when touring overseas.

Also appearing was Peggy O'Keefe, an Australian who had come to Britain in 1960. In 1962, she signed a contract with the Reo Stakis hotel group and came to Glasgow to take up residency for six months in the Chevalier Casino. Peggy stayed for 6 years at the Casino. In the later years of her career she worked as an accompanist for Kenneth, so there was a close association which was clearly evident during Peggy's appearance in the show.

Kenneth relaxed during the programme and particularly enjoyed having Moira and Peggy with him on 'This is Your Life'.

Chapter 9

These Were a Few of His Favourite Things

Land of Heart's Desire

From his album 'The Songs of the Hebrides', Kenneth had a particular favourite, 'Land of Heart's Desire'. He found this song evoked haunting memories to those who were leaving their home land for the last time and sailing off to the new world.

The Album 'Land O' Heart's Desire'.

What a critic has said "Good songs sung by a great performer. If you are looking for a near perfect tenor solo, the title track is it. Kenneth's rendition of 'Land O' Heart's Desire', is a lesson in superb vocal technique. Everything from voice, pitch, phrasing - right down to the last perfectly graduated diminuendo is just about flawless. It is rare to find singing of this calibre outside of opera."

'How Vain is Man'

Of the many recording Kenneth made one of his favourites was 'How Vain is Man' from Judas Maccabaeus by Handel.

Travelogue programmes

Kenneth had fond memories of making four fifty minute travelogue programmes for the BBC. The first was the Road to the Isles followed by 'The Long Islands'

which was about the Outer Hebrides.   The third
programme explored the route of the Jacobite rebellion
and finally a programme featuring the Naples area
entitled 'To Naples'.

St Andrew's Halls

When asked what his favourite concert hall was, he
considered that the old St. Andrew's hall in Glasgow
was his favourite.   The hall had special acoustics
and no amplification was required.   The great Italian
tenor Beniamino Gigli considered the St. Andrew hall
the best he had ever sung in.

Kenneth recalled in 1951 hearing Gigli then in his
sixties singing at the St. Andrew's hall, for ninety
minutes, and that exciting musical experience was what
he referred to as the tingle factor, as Gigli sang.

The St. Andrew's halls were situated at Charing Cross
in Glasgow.   The grand hall could hold 4,500 people.
The halls were built by private funding in 1887 and in
1890 were purchased by the then Glasgow Town
Council.   Unfortunately in 1962 the halls were almost
totally destroyed   by fire and only the Granville Street
façade survived.   An extension to the Mitchell Library
now occupies the eastern part of the site.

Scotland's National Anthem

When it comes to favouring what should be Scotland's National Anthem, Kenneth had very definite views.   He felt that the 'Flower of Scotland' was looking back and not inspiring.   He had watched a Scotland Rugby team singing 'Flower of Scotland' at Murrayfield before a game against England.   He felt that the words and sentiment of the song did not fire up the team at the start of the game.

Instead he favoured 'Scotland the Brave' by Cliff Hanley, who wrote the lyrics to the song in 1951.   Cliff was a Scottish journalist, writer, author, songwriter, historian and broadcaster,a man of many, many parts. The song was written for the singer Robert Wilson who needed a song to close his act at a Christmas Scottish review musical show at the Glasgow Empire.   The song became popular and was quickly adopted by some as the unofficial National Anthem.   Cliff died in 1999 but 'Scotland the Brave' lives on in the hearts of many Scots.

The words of the song are included below: -
Scotland the Brave

Hark when the night is falling
Hear! hear the pipes are calling,
Loudly and proudly calling,
Down thru' the glen.

There where the hills are sleeping,
Now feel the blood a- leaping,
High as the spirits of the old Highland men.

Chorus
Towering   in gallant fame
Scotland my moutain hame,
High may your proud standards gloriously wave,
Land of the high endeavour,
Land of the shining river ,
Land of my heart forever,
Scotland the Brave.

High in the misty Highlands,
Out by the purple islands,
Brave are the hearts that beat
Beneath Scottish skies,
Wild are the wind to meet you,
Staunch are the hearts to greet you,
Kind as the love that shines from fair maidens eyes.
Chorus

Far off in sun-lit places,
Sad are the Scottish faces,
Yearning to feel the kiss.
Of sweet Scottish rain.
Where Tropic skies are beaming,
Love sets the heart a-dreaming,
Longing and dreaming for the homeland again.
Chorus

Scotland will flourish

In the Mail on Sunday dated 22nd May 2011 under the heading 'Revealed the SNP New National Anthem' One wonders what Kenneth McKellar would have felt about this heading. He wasn't greatly enamoured by 'The Flower of Scotland' or by the idea of Scottish independence.

How be it, the official National Anthem, of Scotland is still 'God Save the Queen'. The song the Scottish National Party leader Alex Salmond is calling for to replace this Anthem is 'Scotland will Flourish' written for the folk group the Corries by Ian Richardson who was front man of a band called 'Brocade' and was recorded by the Corries in 1985. The words of the song are as follows

Scotland will Flourish'

1. Scotland will flourish with the sweat of our labour
   The strength of our will and the force of our mind
   Forget the old battles, those days are over
   Hatred corrupts and friendship refines

2. Let the Scots be a nation proud of their heritage
   With an eye to the future and a heart to forgive
   Let us be rid of those bigots and fools
   Who will not let Scotland live and let live

3. Let us govern our country wisely and fairly
   Let each man and woman work with a will
   And Scotland will flourish secure in the knowledge
   That we reap our own harvest and ring our own till

4. And let us be known for our kind hospitality
   A hand that is openly proper to friends
   A hard working people proud and unbending
   Scotland will thrive and win out in the end

5. Scotland will flourish with the sweat of our labour
   The strength of our will and the force of our mind
   Forget the old battles, those days are over
   Hatred corrupts and friendship refines

6. And let us be known for our kind hospitality
   A hand that is openly proper to friends
   A hard working people proud and unbending
   Scotland will thrive and win out in the end

The song seems to be very wordy and whether it would catch on and become as popular as 'Flower of Scotland' only the future will tell.

Alex Salmond gave the song a new and wider audience as he quoted from it, during his election victory speech and again at the Scottish Parliament on the 18th May 2011. He quoted as follows " Let the Scots be a nation proud of their heritage, with an eye to the future and a heart to forgive. Sentiments which Kenneth would have endorsed. An eye to the future will allow us to see whether this forgotten folk song gains prominence and and becomes Scotland's National Anthem.

Favourite Singers and Influences

Richard Tauber 1891 - 1948

Richard a tenor was among Kenneth's favourite singers. He was born Ernst Seiffert in Austria. His father was half - Jewish and had to flee from Austria and Germany to Britain where   he made his permanent home. Richard completed a total of 735 commercial recordings which included opera, operetta, art songs, popular tunes and novelties.

Paul Robeson 1898 - 1976

Paul was a base baritone, born in New Jersey. His father was a former slave, the Reverend William Robeson. He was widely recognised for his singing from the musical   'Showboat' where he changed the lines of the song 'Old Man River'. Robeson's legacy has been an inspiration to millions around the world. His courageous stance against opposition and inequality in part led to the civil rights movement of the 1960s. Through his stage and film performances, he opened doors to inter-racial performances. With his travels across America and abroad he opened the world's eyes to opposition. Robeson stood tall and proud against governmental and societal forces. He remains in the memory as successful scholar, athlete, performer and activist.

Both Richard and Paul were favourites and great influences on Kenneth from boyhood and were in his opinion 'Lovely singers'.

Peter Dawson   1882 - 1965

Peter was an Australian Bass Baritone who gained world wide renown through song recitals and many best selling recordings of Operatic Arias. Peter made a well loved recording of 'Waltzing Matilda' which as it happened, Kenneth had chosen for a ring tone for his mobile phone. His opinion was that Peter was wonderful as he had the kind of voice that could be identified within the first four bars which was similar to Kenneth's voice. In 1984 Dawson was chosen by the Guinness Book of Recorded Sound as one of the top ten singers on disc, of all time, listed alongside such luminaries as Elvis Presley and the great operatic tenor Enrico Caruso.

Quite an Accolade
Peter Dawson's influence was felt   in Kenneth's professional life as a singer.   All three of these great singers left their mark on him and helped him to become the greatest Scottish Tenor, each was very different but had one thing in common, great talent.

The Corran Hall, Oban
Besides taking part in summer shows at the Queens Hall in Dunoon, Kenneth participated in shows at the Winter Gardens in Rothesay, The Gaiety in Ayr, and often at the Corran Hall in Oban.   Hedy travelled to Oban with him, they made a day of it, they arrived in Oban in time for the afternoon rehearsal, and enjoyed meal together before the evening show.   He enjoyed doing a summer season at the Corran Hall.   The summer of 1991was his thirteenth successive summer at this location.

Sailing By
After Kenneth had finished the show they would travel back to Glasgow, as they travelled they would enjoy listening to Radio 4.   They would gauge how well they were doing time-wise as they hoped to be approaching Loch Lomond-side as 'Sailing By' came over the Radio. Sailing By is the music played prior to the reading of the shipping forecast at 12.45am.   Providing there were no unseen delays they would be back at their Glasgow home by 2.00am.   It had been a long day but both Ken and Hedy were keen to   be back at home.

'Sailing By' was written by Ronald Binge who Kenneth knew.   Ronald wrote light music notably 'Elizabethan Serenade'   and made an arrangement of 'Charmaine' for the Mantovani's   Orchestra.   'Sailing By' its function on Radio 4 is to fill any air time, between the late reading at approximately 12.45am and the Shipping Forecast at 12.48am, which mariner's rightly expect to be transmitted precisely on schedule.

Kenneth McKellar at the Gaiety in Ayr May 1954

At the beginning of May 1954 the Popplewells who had bought the Gaiety Theatre back in 1925 and, who operated the theatre till 1973, created the famous 'Gaiety Whirl' Summer Reviews   They had noted and been concerned about the decline of Robert Wilson's voice who at the time was a leading Scottish tenor.   In 1954 Robert Wilson   was 47 years old and approaching that age of 50, when it was considered that a tenor's voice could go into decline.

In the week commencing May 24th 1954   a new tenor was to take early steps on the national stage , none other than Kenneth McKellar.   He would go on to thrill millions for decades to come and prove an exception to the rule that tenors voices decline when they reach the age of 50, sometimes called the 'rule of 50'.   In 1954, the Popplewells reckoned that Kenneth was 'Very good but inexperienced.'

At the Gaiety in May 1978
Kenneth McKellar after an absence of 24 years, returned to the Gaiety to star for a month from 22nd May 1978 with a programme change half-way through. The Popplewell family no longer owned the theatre.   It was now run by a local authority management.
 Like all great artists his performance was an

education, the sound level at all points in the auditorium from the front stalls to the back balcony was perfect. His act lasted exactly the same time every performance to the split minute.

The Show was entitled 'McKellar and Friends' and the latter were comedian Ron Dale, Juggler Judy Moxon. Ian Muir, Louise Kelly and the Brian Seivwright Dancers headed by Brian himself, and Isabel James. Kenneth was a source of good press copy, a comedy script writer a children's story writer, a baker of bread and a motor cyclist.

In the *Gaiety Chit Chat* , a piece for   the paper on June 9th 1978   was about the possibility of a black clad 'ton up kid' swooping along Carrick Street as Ayr shops were shutting and the traffic was easing homeward, and this would be Scotlands' greatest tenor arriving for work .   He had used the bike during numerous summer shows in England but he had said it was unlikely in Ayr as he was currently suffering from conjunctivitis. However on the last night Saturday 17th June 1978 before the first house started he said   "If you like to take a look over at 'Youngs Garage' you will see the bike."   And there it was 1000cc 4 cylinder shaft driven, water cooled Honda.   He had made the story come true, travelling all the way from his home in the Glasgow area.   What a Pro!   Young's Garage was a prominent local landmark opposite the front of the Gaiety

Earlier in the run, one night in a serious reflective mood he remarked "I wouldn't like to be starting again. There are very few theatres and the advent of the microphone has killed a lot of singers. And then there is the question of television. If it is bad television, you are better not to do it, if it is good television you can get so much exposure that you will go out of fashion very quickly."
Source "The Gaiety" by John Moore

The Harley Davidson - A Passion

Kenneth gained an interest for motor bikes while in England, and in particular, he had a passion for Harley Davidsons, the Mercedes of motor-bikes. When Kenneth moved back to Scotland he found the motor bike a way of getting about quickly, particularly getting round Loch Lomond-side and up into the Highlands.

The Haylie Brae

Only once did Kenneth come off his bike and that was on the Haylie Brae just outside Largs. He came off his bike due to a spillage of oil on the road next to the Largs cemetery. The accident caused him to land on his chest but no serious damage was done. Despite being shaken up, what happened next made Kenneth's day. When he came off the bike a man coming behind in car stopped and came over and asked Ken "Are you all right, son?" He was about 65 years at the time but with the helmet it was difficult to see what age he was.

In 1997 Ken sold his beloved Harley Davidson but in 1998 he was looking at two other bikes with a view to replacing the Harley. Ask if he was a good mechanic said "With the help of a battery of good mechanics I have kept the bike on the road".

A Song for Everyone

Kenneth introduced his programmes on Radio and Television with a 'Song for Everyone' which was written by Cliff Hanley, the words of the song are as follows
'A Song for Everyone'
Chorus
My song is all that I can bring to you,
My song is all I call my own,
My song may bring a breath of spring to you,
I sing to you and you alone.

My song will tell you how I cling to you,
Although we may be far apart,
You are the word and music of my melody,
For in my song is all my heart .

I look for you in every lonely lane,
In every crowded street,
In my heart I keep a glad refrain
To give you when we meet.
Chorus

As Kenneth looked back on a 'Song for Everyone' , with Eddie Fraser being the producer of the show for the BBC each week the format for the show was two operatic pieces, two Scots songs, one operetta piece and one popular song.

When Kenneth reflected on what he had to prepare for each show He felt he must have been out of his mind to follow the above format which involved learning thousands of songs over a period of years. Yet it was good training and made him discipline himself to be properly prepared for each week's show.

Admirer of Robert Burns

Kenneth was a great admirer of Robert Burns. He had recorded many of his songs   and his 'Songs of Robert Burns' album, remains the definitive one. He was Honorary President and life member of most of the Principle Burns Clubs world wide, and this included The Burns and Pushkin club in Moscow.

He always said that Burns was great for him. He pleaded that "People would leave Burns alone and listen to what he was saying and how he said it."
His preference was just to concentrate on the skill and beauty of   his writing, his songs and poetry which were really a great joy to Kenneth.

From a Young Age

From his notes on the album 'Songs of Robert Burns' he wrote "Since I was two years of age, the songs of Burns have been as much a part of my discovery of music as were the 'Doh-Ray-Me' learned at school in Paisley. I heard them from the lips of my grandparents, sung by my father, and at the knee of my mother. So unlike learning early piano pieces, the learning of Burns songs was very natural, tremendously enjoyable, and resulted in a love of them which cannot die, the same love as the Scots have for the Trossachs, Loch Lomond and the mystic islands of the Hebrides."

Doing Burns Songs Justice.

Kenneth had the ability to reach the full range required to do Burns songs justice. He regularly attended Burns Suppers to sing, and to appreciate Burns as a speaker regaled the Immortal Memory. In 2009 he was excited when Burns was voted 'The Greatest Scot' by the Scottish public in a vote which was run by the Scottish Television Channel STV.

Influences

Burns listed as a main influence in his life one Robert Ferguson who became known a Scotland's forgotten poet.

In turn all of the following have been influenced in their work by Robert Burns

Charlotte Bronte	**Novelist and Poet**
John Clare	**Poet**
Samuel Taylor Coleridge	**Poet**
Percy Bysshe Shelley	**Poet**
Bob Dylan	**Poet/ singer/songwriter**
James Whitcomb Riley	**Children's Poet**
Frank Lebby Stanton	**Poet and Lyricist**
John Steinbeck	**Writer**
William Wordsworth	**Poet**
JD Salinger	**Novelist**
James Joyce	**Novelist**

And of course   Kenneth McKellar .
Quite a list to be influenced by the humble Scots farmer, poet, lyricist and finally excise man at Dumfries.

Robert Burns Birthplace Museum

On the first of December 2010 an exciting event took place with the opening of the Robert Burns Birthplace Museum at Alloway near Ayr, by the National Trust for Scotland, under the publicity heading of 'Discover your Genius'.   Kenneth would have loved this Museum.
In all,   the museum   comprises   of   Burns Cottage, Alloway Auld Kirk, Brig   O' Doon, Poets Path, Burns Monument, and the new Birthplace Museum.

A Popular Scottish Love Song
My Love is Like a Red, Red Rose

Kenneth's version was sung in D Flat and he described the song story as a love destined not to end, the song transcends time and it touches people from all walks of life.

Origins of the Song

The song was first published in 1790's and there is a fascinating story behind its publication.
Several publishers wanted to publish the song, as recording labels would do today.   In 1794 Pietor Urbani published the song in a 'Collection of Scots Songs'.   He claimed he had collaborated with Burns, but Burns denied that he had done so.   Urbani was part of a thriving Italian community in Edinburgh in the late
18th century.

James   Johnstone published the first three stanzas of the song in the 'Scots Musical Museum' in 1797.   The song was to be sung to the tune ' Major Graham' by Neil Gow.   It was a fiddle tune and difficult to sing. As far as Kenneth was concerned when someone referred to a 'popular'   Scottish song , the song that immediately came to his mind, and he made so popular was   'My Love is Like a Red, Red Rose'.

Finally George Thomson published the tune in his original Scottish Airs in 1799 and set the song to the tune 'Wishaw's Favourites', again the tune was challenging to sing.

Later the melody to which the song is now sung became the most popular version with a tune called 'Low Down in the Broom'which Robert Archibald Smith matched with Burns words in 1820.   Robert published the song in his 'Scottish Minstrel' in 1821 and the tune first appeared in the 'Caledonian Pocket Companion'.

Robert and his family moved to Paisley in 1800 where Robert and his father worked as muslin weavers. Robert became a friend of the poet Robert Tannahill who helped him to get into music which was his real interest.   He became a teacher of music and 1807   he was appointed a leader of the Psalmody at Paisley Abbey, and soon was able to form a excellent choir and pursue a career he loved and was talented at.

<u>Those who have been influenced by 'My Love is like a Red, Red Rose,'</u>

Bob Dylan
Bob Dylan has claimed that this Burns song was the main source of his creative inspiration.

Eddi Reader (singer and songwriter)
The Burns story became a part of Eddi Readers' life when she was asked to sing 'My Love is like a Red, Red Rose' on a TV production for Burns night.   While learning the song something important happened to

Eddi, she felt that she had been singing the song all her life and it was like an old friend coming home to her.

When she came to record the song with an orchestra to give Burns words and tune the magnificence they deserve she sought out non classical musicians who would have represented the musicians that Burns would have played with himself in the bars of Ayrshire. Eddie wanted to send Burns a message, to show him how loved and cherished his words and ideas have endured.

Source - Legacy of Burns by Eddi Reader , Robert Burns Birthplace Museum Guide.

Permissions

Permissions for the words of the songs included in chapters 8 and 9 are as follows.

'The Midges'   See Chapter 8   and 'The Pan Drap' song see Chapter 8   composed by Kenneth McKellar and reproduced with permission of the ISA Music Publishing.

'Scotland the Brave' see chapter 9.   Reproduced with permission of the copyright holders Kerr's Music Corporation Ltd.

'Scotland will Flourish' see Chapter 9 .   Reproduced with permission of the copyright holders Corries (Music) Ltd.

'A Song for Everyone' see Chapter 9.   Extensive efforts have been made to identify and seek permission to reproduce the words of this song, this included contact with Music lawyers and copyright lawyers.

Chapter 10

Reflections of a Long Time Friend

The following are reflections by Joe Campbell, formerly Managing Director of West Sound Radio in Ayr and a long time friend of Kenneth McKellar.

Character of the Man

Perhaps the character of the man explains much of what the man achieved and how. Ken, as his friends knew him, was a very private man who did not make friends easily, nor did he set out to make friends. If that suggests he was in any way unfriendly, then that would be wrong, but he very much preferred to relax with a few people, carefully chosen and trusted as he was not in any way gregarious despite his musical talent and success.

Many musicians who toured the world with Ken over a long number of years, have said that although they liked him immensely, they never really got to know him. He always held something in reserve, except for this small coterie of his nearest and dearest, when he would relax totally .

He had a fine sense of humour, sometimes wicked but never malevolent and rarely did he speak ill of fellow performers. He rarely showed emotion on stage as he often said that to do so would have its effect on his voice and this is completely understandable. However he was in tears as he watched the Love Duet from La Boheme sung by Renata Tebaldi and Jussi Bjorling.

When Hedy, his Swiss-born wife, died at the age of 61, Kenneth was devastated and perhaps showed a vulnerability which although unexpected was endearing. He was very fond of Joe's wife as she, like him couldn't pretend. He was devoid of pretension, and Joe often thought "You really don't know how good you are."

He won the Henry Leslie prize for singing when at the Royal Academy of Music in London and this brought him to the attention of the BBC for whom he began broadcasting Scots songs in 1947. It also brought him to the notice of Dame Moura Lympany who contacted him and ask if he would sing, to her accompaniment, a World War 1 song extolling the benefits of X-ray, and entitled 'The New Photograph-ee!'
She wanted the song privately recorded for a birthday party being held for Winston Churchill. When Churchill heard it, Ken told Joe all he said was "I think I'll remember it." Lesser singers would have claimed that Churchill waxed eloquent on the beauty of the singing but not Kenneth McKellar.

Dame Moura Lympany was born in Cornwall, Mary Johnston. Moura is a Russian diminutive for Mary, and with her origins being Cornish, Lympany is an old Cornish name. She was a pianist who was referred to, as 'a Virtuoso of Dreaming'. When she appeared on Desert island Discs she chose her own recordings as she stated " My records are so damn good".

Character of the Voice

Like the man this was a voice which was unadorned. Kenneth did not have a big voice, not even a voice which could ring top register, but a beautiful voice which was even from middle C to top B.   His diction was impeccable because he always believed in telling a story and although he was obviously highly trained, his training was never uppermost in the listeners' awareness as he sounded so natural.   Hear him sing "Sound an Alarm" from Judas Maccabaeus and then hear him sing 'Oh My Love is Like a Red Red Rose' and you will hear the pure singing which conceals the technique behind it.   That was Ken's art.

Sir Jimmy Shand

Kenneth was a man without pretension and he used to be bemused by the honours system which often glorified a motley bunch of people with little or no right to accept an honour for doing their job.   It is well known although he never spoke of it, that Kenneth turned down the offer of an Honour which would be in character.. The Honour was an OBE and the offer was made in 1992.

Kenneth returned from his daughter's home which was then in Australia a few weeks after Jimmy Shand had received his Honour, and became Sir Jimmy, he phoned Joe Campbell.   He felt he would like to pay Jimmy a visit at Auchtermuchty to congratulate him personally and, knowing that Joe had sung on Television and Radio with Jimmy, and wondered if Joe would go with him. Auchtermuchty is a Royal Burgh and a Historical town nestling in the hills of the north - east of Fife.

They met Jimmy at 11.00am at his home and as always he was prepared, immaculate in a white shirt and tie, cardigan, newly pressed trousers and a pair of slippers. Without a doubt Kenneth and Jimmy were the most taciturn undemonstrative of Scots and yet they embraced emotionally and the next few hours flew past as they reminisced. Joe asked Jimmy at one point when Ken was out of the room, "How good was he Jimmy?" And the reply "Juist the best,son, juist the best." No more needed to be said. Ken had a funny story about Jimmy and it concerned their first broadcast when Ken was to sing 'The Song of the Clyde.' Ken said " I'll sing it in D flat Mr Shand." To which came back the reply "Suit yersel' laddie but I'll be playin' it in the key of C."

Chapter 11

After Seventy

After Seventy

When Kenneth reached the age of seventy, he made a number of decisions
Singing... The first of these and most important was that he would retire from performing, which had been his life for the past fifty years. He had travelled and worked all over the British Isles and overseas and his tremendous accomplishments have been detailed in earlier chapters. It was time to slow down and enjoy the fruits of his hard work, and also to appreciate the esteem he was held in by so many people all over the world.

Biking... the second decision was to give up his motor-bike, at that time he had a BMW 80. He loved the freedom the motor bike had given him. and he had travelled all over the United Kingdom and particularly to the Oban area which he loved. On the continent he travelled regularly to Switzerland, to visit his wife Hedy's family and also to Germany , France and Italy. On one occasion Jimmy McGregor asked "Does your wife not object to your going away on the motor-bike?" to this Kenneth replied "Indeed not, she encourages me to go."

Baking ...
Kenneth tried but neither enjoyed or excelled at playing golf. Instead he found that the three hours he would spend on the golf-course, could be much more

productively used in baking. In three hours he could bake four loaves which he both enjoyed baking and eating.

Singing at Harry's funeral

When Kenneth's oldest brother Harry passed away his widow asked him if he would sing at the funeral service. At first he was very hesitant about singing, because of the emotion of the occasion. Kenneth sang 'God be in your head' and sang it beautifully and everyone present was moved by his performance, with tears all round.

After the service the family stood in line to shake hands with those who had attended. As they became older Kenneth and his other brother Jimmy looked very like each other. One of the congregation came up to Jimmy and expressed great appreciation for his singing. Jimmy thanked him but no mention that he wasn't the singer. When the man reached Kenneth he quickly passed saying very little. Afterwards both Kenneth and Jimmy had a really good laugh about the incident.

"Mr McKellar You will be singing at my funeral".

Kenneth lived for many years in the West End of Glasgow, and one day he went into an ironmongers in the Anniesland area. Just after he entered the shop an elderly couple came in. The lady immediately recognised Kenneth, and engaged him in conversation.

She said "Mr McKellar, you'll be singing at my funeral." Kenneth was a bit taken aback and asked what he was to sing, she replied "My favourite is 'How Great Thou Art', do you know that hymn?" Kenneth said he did and went on to ask "When will the funeral be?" the lady was not fazed by that question and said "In due course, and my family will be in touch with you". The couple then left the shop, and the man behind the counter stood with his mouth open, and couldn't but hear the conversation and wondered if he was believing what he was hearing.

Birthday Surprise…

Kenneth was stuck for words when his record company sprang a surprise seventieth birthday party in his honour in Glasgow. Lismor Record chiefs invited him for a birthday treat. When he arrived, a host of friends and acquaintances were there to greet him, and Lismor presented him with Platinum, Gold and Solver discs in recognition of his world wide sales.

Retiring from a busy singing schedule…

Kenneth had lived a very busy life, at one time he was performing shows throughout the British Isles, and in between times travelled to London to record the Handel Arias with Sir Adrian Boult. He was a devoted family man and when he wasn't travelling in Britain or overseas, he was happy to be at home in the West End of Glasgow.

In retirement he performed from time to time, but his whole pace of life had slowed down. After the death of his wife, he was keen to spend time with his children and grandchildren. His son Kenneth lived in London, a city he was familiar with from his time at the Royal College of Music. His son and family subsequently moved to Switzerland, the birthplace of his mother and their grandmother Hedy, who had family in both Switzerland and Germany.

However Kenneth didn't desert music entirely as he still enjoyed playing the piano and writing arrangements and orchestrations. He did all the orchestrations for his last five albums and he found it very stimulating. He talked about looking out the window of his home and jotting down ideas and that it was hard work, but on hearing the notes being played was very rewarding.

<u>To Daughter Jane's…</u>

In Sydney
Jane and her family moved to Australia in the late 1980s and Kenneth made frequent visits. He was intrigued by the Australian accents of his two lovely grand-daughters Hedy and Callie. Callie was named after the family's favourite island on the west coast of Scotland , Callanish. They both called their grandfather 'Pop'.

Kenneth enjoyed his visits, he appreciated the company of his family, and was fascinated by Sydney and the surrounding area of New South Wales, and he wished he had his Harley Davidson with him.

To Lake Tahoe...
Jane and her husbands business took them to live near Lake Tahoe. Lake Tahoe is in part in the state of California which is the part the family lived in, and part in the state of Nevada, and is a beautiful area. The lake is 22 miles long and 12 miles wide and is a lovely part of the world to live in.

Kenneth regularly visited the family.   The accents of his grand-daughters changed to reflect   their new life in America.   There was much to discover and the motor bike would have been a great asset.   In fact Kenneth spent most of the last few years of his life staying with Jane and her family.

Chapter 12

Obituaries, Appreciations and
The Memorial Service

Scots Tenor McKellar dies aged 82

Kenneth's passing …
Jane , Kenneth daughter stated "My father's illness came on very quickly, it was all very, very sudden, so his death came as a great shock.   He was able to keep his spirits up and have a sense of humour and a warm personality right up to the end, so that was a great blessing."

Kenneth died just a week after being diagnosed as having pancreatic cancer at the age of 82, at Jane's home near Lake Tahoe, California, on the 9th April 2010.   He was born in Paisley on the 23rd June 1927. In 1953 he married the Swiss born Hedy, who tragically died of a heart attack in 1990.   The couple had a son Kenneth and daughter Jane, and were blessed with five grandchildren.

Jane McKellar, Kenneth's daughter said "I hope people will remember him for the breadth of the music he made.   He also had a great sense of humour.   He was a very private person, so for someone who spent so much of time in the public eye, when he was off stage , he was an intensely private person. His singing was effortless and concealed the huge talent that made it so.   Those who knew him best remember a man of great humour, a man who would not bear pretentiousness and who, although not able to suffer fools gladly was totally without conceit.

Alex Salmond

Paying Tribute to Kenneth McKellar, the Scottish First Minister Alex Salmond said "No one is irreplaceable but it is likely that there will ever be another Kenneth McKellar. As well as being an outstanding entertainer with a magnificent voice, he also had a deep commitment to helping the careers of young performers. It should also be remembered that he commanded a huge international audience, and took the songs of Scotland world wide. He is a great loss to music and the country and will be sorely missed at home and abroad."

Source BBC News   09/04/2010

An article in the Paisley Daily Express on Friday April 16th 2010   under the heading

'Scottish Parliament honours Kenneth McKellar'

Politicians have paid tribute to singing star Kenneth McKellar. Mr McKellar, from Paisley, died on Friday April 9th , at his daughter Jane's home near Lake Tahoe USA.   Bill Wilson, MSP for the West of Scotland , tabled a motion at the Scottish parliament, honouring Mr. McKellar life and work. He said " I was very sad to hear of the passing of this great man who like myself was born in Paisley. As a keen hill-walker and Scots speaker I greatly appreciated his music which echoes my love of Scotland's great outdoors and culture. Mr McKellar contributed to the promotion of the Scot's language by bringing the songs of Burns into Scottish home through television programmes such as the 'White Heather Club' .I think it is important to remember that although he was primarily known for his musical prowess, he also was an environmentalist. He will be held in fond memory by Scots around the world. He has left an important legacy and he will be remembered as a man who appreciated Scotland's language, her music and her unique natural environment."

Taken from the Scots Blog Awards site for "Go Lassie Go"
<u>Obituary of Kenneth McKellar, Scotland's Finest</u> <u>Tenor   by Sarah Nelson</u>

The notes on the CD of Kenneth McKellar's memorable recording with George McPhee and the choir of Paisley Abbey talk of hymns and sacred music by 'That most beloved of tenors.'

<u>Finest singer of Scot's Songs</u>

To most Scots over sixty- five and to numerous expatriates living abroad, and to many classical musicians, singers, and classical music critics, he was the finest singer of Scots music of his era, still billed today on radio stations as 'The Great Scottish Tenor'. His 'Messiah' recording with Joan Sutherland remains one of Decca's all time biggest sellers. American critic,

Richard Munro, described McKellar " One of the great tenors that the twentieth century has produced, who as the interpreter of Burns songs and the Lowland Scot's traditions was without peer."

Great Mastery

Kenneth combined great mastery of technique and beauty of sound with an unusual feeling and sensitivity for everything he sang. Technical mastery was put at the service of that feeling, not the other way round.

Countertenor

He performed with powerful impact unaccompanied 'She moves through the fair to spare drumbeats.' His religious works ranged to great power to great sensitivity as on the brief, incomparable 'God be in my Head'. His show tunes and musicals contrast with a stunning interpretation of Britten's 'Down by the Salley Gardens.' which suggests he could have been an equally successful countertenor. (A countertenor is a male singing voice whose vocal range is equivalent to that of a contralto, mezzo-soprano).

It is to be hoped that at last, the younger generation of Scots will listen to his works, that his admirers will ensure all his best work is re-mastered and featured once more in record stores, and that his reputation can finally be re-established as one of Scotland's greatest ever singers

Kenneth McKellar - Lost in the White Heather

Sources - Living Scotsman.com 24/11/2010 by Sarah Nelson

Listening to Kenneth

My generation rejected anyone 'old fashioned,' high brow or kilted, and embraced Mo-town and Soul. So, apart from admiring McKellar's best known songs like the Eriskay Love Lilt, I'd never really sat down to listen to him singing.

I was spurred on to investigate, by learning that my late aunt, the pioneering Scottish BBC broadcaster, Elizabeth Adair invited Kenneth for his first radio broadcast while a forestry student in Aberdeen. I bought a couple of Kenneth's CDs last month. Recent digital mastering of his CDs has brought his rich voice, buried on scratch vinyl inside many a faded LP cover, to a wide audience again.

Re-releasing Albums

Re-released albums, powerful and poignant to hear, include the acclaimed songs of Robert Burns(Now combined on a CD with the Songs of the Hebrides). The Decca years from 1955 to 1980 and the sacred music recorded from Paisley Abbey, and Kenneth's Book of Hymns, are all marvellous examples of McKellar's musical output. These are albums to dip into, for some song types will not interest everyone. It feels unimaginable that songs such as 'Mary Morrison',

'The Sheiling Song', 'Flow Gently Sweet Afton', 'Eilidh Dear', and 'God be in My Head', could ever be sung better or more movingly than this, its extraordinary how he makes old numbers like 'My Ain Folk' sound unbearably poignant.

Little Played

It feels utterly wrong that Kenneth could be so often underrated and little played today. How did this happen? Barely known by the younger Scottish public, he hardly features ever on the copious Scottish compilation CDs sold to tourists. It is in strong contrast to the professionals he worked with, like the Irish singer Patricia Cahill, who more than thirty years ago collaborated with Kenneth on the great duets album.

In No-man's Land

As a result, American collector Kevin D'Arcy said "He suffered from being in no-man's land. Most of the classical world ignored him because he chose not to pursue a career in opera or classical music and the 'folkies' thought him too 'hi-falutin' for their tastes. Scots folk music was moving away to very different song styles, while the Gaelic tradition had been firmly guarded. Today, crossovers and /or twin careers involving classical and other musical genres proves much more acceptable for a host of singers and musicians.

Without Honour

Does Kenneth McKellar expose the fact that, as a nation, we are still unsure how highly we really respect all swathes of our own music and song tradition, feeling more comfortable when we either are lampooning it or turning it into loud thumping rock ?   Surely, its time to shed prejudice, and judge his music's quality for ourselves.   High time, too, for our politicians, especially an SNP government, to ask how on earth Scotland's greatest tenor, a definitive Burns interpreter, and a gracious ambassador for the country for decades could remain without honour.   Kenneth did turn down an honour of an OBE several years ago and I hope our singers and musicians add their support that Alex Salmond should hasten round now and honour him, at the same speed with which he used to roam around Europe on his BMW motor-bike.

Comments by the Author

Sarah Nelson's views as expressed in the above article under the heading 'Kenneth McKellar - Lost in the White Heather', reflects the fact that the younger generations have turned away from the image of Scottish music as presented by Kenneth, Jimmy Shand etc.

The TV Hogmany shows have changed and portray a different image of Scotland and seem to be influenced by the English and American promotion of music.   Yet there is a place and a market for the kind of Scottish entertainment Kenneth and Andy Stewart provided, and as Sarah has stated there is a need to have the music of Kenneth McKellar more available for the Scottish public   and tourists alike to be exposed to and enjoy.

What the Fans Have Said

Source Obituary on Kenneth McKellar   - The Telegraph

Alan Bonney
Stated "Kenneth McKellar was one of the true giants of Scottish popular music.   I was sad to learn of his passing.   My mum has a ton of old vinyls by him and I still enjoy his music."

Dennis Logie
He stated " What a marvellous voice, now stilled. I learned so much about my Scottish heritage from his music. He opened doors for me."

James Brock
He stated   " Another icon and favourite son of Scotland has gone.   Kenneth and Andy Stewart made me proud to be Scottish .   I am sure that Andy will be waiting for Kenneth at Heaven's gate.   Thanks for the memories, Laddie Rest Well."

Heather Abraham
Says "I remember my parents taking me to a navy day in Scotland and being introduced to Kenneth. His voice was beautiful and the many and varied songs he sang were a joy to hear. My father especially loved to hear Kenneth sing. My mum had him on her favourites list. Hogmany is not the same since he and Andy Stewart are not there to bring in the New Year."

John Rayner
Kenneth was one of my all time favourite tenors. I don't think that anyone can match his unaccompanied singing of 'She Walked to the Fair'.

M. Lyons
Kenneth was my mother's favourite singer. Having grown up on hearing him, he became one of mine. When my mother suffered from dementia at the end of her life and no longer recognised faces, her face still lit up when she heard his tones. He was a wonderful singer. His rendition of 'God Be in My Head' produces goose pimples when I hear it.

Susan A. Carey
Kenneth McKellar was my mother's favourite singer, she played his albums every day, at home and in the car. We would have played them all the way up to our regular holidays in Oban to see the man himself perform in the Corran Halls, Oban.

Nesta

So sorry to say goodbye to a lovely singer.   He had been a favourite in our family for the last forty years, and no recordings of Scottish songs will ever match his exquisite renderings, particularly those orchestrated by Bob Sharples.   We are so lucky that modern recordings can immortalise such a superb voice if not (alas, the delightful person who owned it)

K.M. Keegan

Many years ago Kenneth produced an album of Irish music which became one of my Irish Mother's favourites.   I enjoyed it too and often performed some of them in front of my drunken friends.   ' The Star of County Down' and   'The Garden where the Praties Grow' were my favourites.

To Scotia's Minstrel

Ron Deen who at one time worked as a civil engineer for the old Paisley Burgh, was a great admirer of Kenneth. He wrote a poetic tribute to him dubbed 'To Scotia's Minstrel'.   Ron stated " I attended a lot of his concerts and introduced myself afterwards, I was always impressed by him and I was one of his many, many loyal followers

Appreciation by Fellow Professionals

Anne Lorne Gillies

Anne is a Gaelic singer and a gold medallist at the

National Mod , who went onto sing professionally . She worked with Kenneth at the Gaiety in Ayr for a week's season for several years the late 1980s. It was both a happy and successful experience. She recalls," It was a pleasure to work with Kenneth both as a friend and a colleague. He was always a true ambassador for Scotland and attracted huge audiences throughout the world

Bill Innes
Bill's career went from being a crofter to an airline pilot. He is now a broadcaster , and is a Gaelic speaker. Bill was of the opinion that although Kenneth had a strong Paisley accent, when he sang it was a different story. He was immediately recognisable as the years went on, he became very comfortable on stage and when appearing on television.

Professor Chris Underwood,
Head of Vocal Performance at the RSAMD

Professor Underwood analysed Kenneth's voice to find out what was so special about it. He felt, Kenneth always sang the high notes with ease and there was a beauty in his English diction.

There was a flexibility in his voice and he had a real technique and a wide range of repertoire, which was so immediately appealing to the listener. Kenneth never sang in Gaelic as he was honest enough to realise not to invade a territory which was not his.

Paul McCallum
Paul is a singer and Gaelic speaker

What was so special about Kenneth McKellar, was that he had, what is referred to, as 'Voice Identity', In that the listener recognised his voice immediately. An example of Kenneth's voice, was when he sang 'Every Valley Shall Exalt Thee' from Handel, from the first note his voice was like running up and down a ladder. It showed the control of his voice, his breath control and his understanding of this wonderful piece of music.

Margaret Bennett
Singer, Scottish Folklorist and Gaelic Speaker

Kenneth McKellar's voice was wonderful, but it wasn't just his voice, he had a manner and understanding so the songs were very close to his heart.

When I was twelve years old and learning to sing, I remember my mother saying something I didn't understand at the time, she said "You have to get inside the song to sing it". I now know what she was saying, and that's what any singer wants to achieve. If you listen to Kenneth, he achieved this.

Jamie McDougall
Tenor and Broadcaster

Jamie tells that as a student of seventeen at the Douglas Academy of Music and a young tenor, he was given an album of Kenneth McKellar singing Handel's Arias with Adrian Bolt. It was a 'Road to Damascus' moment in Jamie's life. He had no idea Kenneth could sing a wonderful range of Handel's Arias.

It sounded effortless to Kenneth and it was, but behind that impression a lot of work and time had been taken, in preparing and keeping his voice going. Jamie found Kenneth's technique unbelievable, and his voice was a lighter instrument than a lot of singers. He had a range which gave a warmth to his voice, which was very distinctive.

Jamie found it interesting in an interview with Kenneth that it was George Martin of the Beatles fame who steered Kenneth away from Classical music into singing Scottish songs. George had observed that there was no- one doing the 'Scottish Stuff' and if Kenneth concentrate on Scottish songs it would set him apart and start him off on a new career."

Jean Redpath
Singer of Burns' songs and lecturer in folklore.

Singers of Burns' songs from very different traditions appreciate Kenneth brought the works of Burns to an international audience. Jean was thrilled to have had the opportunity to work with him particularly to sing the love songs of Burns.

He believed in what he was singing, It didn't matter what he was wearing or what the audience expected, he was such a talent.

Jean felt she had a slight chip on her shoulder about Kenneth's profile as, " The voice of Scotland in a kilt". She was bowled over that Kenneth was able to sing so well, often in challenging circumstances.

Kathleen MacDonald
Singer and Gaelic Speaker

Kathleen considered that a tenor voice is something that neither a soprano, baritone, or even a bass has.   There is something in their voice that comforts the audience, but which is difficult to explain.   this is especially true when he soars up to the high notes.

Kenneth never disappointed whether he was singing folk songs or traditional songs like 'She Moved Through the Fair'.   He sang it beautifully and of course his renditions of 'My Love is Like a Red,Red Rose', set him apart.   Kathleen reflected that everyone should hear him sing Handel's Messiah.   She never had heard anyone before or after him who could sing Handel's music as well as he could.

Taking into consideration how the music industry is today, Kathleen felt Kenneth wouldn't have been as successful now, as he was at the time of his major achievements.   He was there at the right time, with the right voice.   Audiences enjoyed his singing regardless whether he was singing folk, opera, or classical music

The Memorial Service   Wednesday 30th June 2010

The following report appeared in the Paisley Daily
Express Thursday 1st July 2010 under the heading
'Hundreds pay tribute to the life and legacy of the Scots
singing legend who never forgot his home town.'

Dear Kenneth………. Death cannot take away your
sweet voice.   Report by Kenneth Speirs

Singer Kenneth McKellar is remembered at Paisley
Abbey

Kenneth McKellar
The world-famous tenor who never forgot his home
town of Paisley has been remembered with love and
affection at a special memorial service.
       Hundreds of people went along to the service for

the late Kenneth McKellar at Paisley Abbey – the church where he made many of his most famous recordings.

Ordinary Buddies mingled with showbiz stars and figures from public life to remember the entertainer who was one of Scotland's most famous sons.

His daughter Jane told the packed church: "My father never forgot who he was or where he was from. "Paisley, Scotland and this Abbey were very close to his heart."

Recordings by Mr McKellar, as well as music he had written, were played at the touching service.

There was absolute silence as a vintage recording by the singer and soprano Patricia Cahill of Robert Burns' great song on heartbroken love 'Ae Fond Kiss' was played.

And there were tears as one of his finest Burns' recordings, 'My Love is Like a Red, Red Rose,' filled the ancient Abbey.

The Burns theme continued as the church echoed to the sound of 'Auld Lang Syne' being recited by Mr McKellar's great friend, the actor and director Tom Fleming.

And there was laughter too as a succession of people recalled the man they were very proud to call a friend.

Dr Bill Hall remembered how he and his friend Kenneth – a very private man who was famous the length and breadth of Scotland – travelled to Edinburgh for a speaking engagement.

"We parked the car at Waverley Station and Ken went into the boot and brought out a Crombie coat, a black Homburg hat and very thick sunglasses," recalled Dr Hall.

"I said 'What on earth is it? Fancy dress? He said, 'No, I can't stand people staring at me!'"

Dr Hall quoted, with a small adaptation, the poem Heraclitus, by Victorian poet William Cory.

He said: "They told me, Kenneth, they told me you were dead. They brought me bitter news to hear and bitter tears to shed. I wept as I remembered how often you and I had tired the sun with talking and sent him down the sky."

"And now that thou art lying, my dear old Carian guest, a handful of grey ashes, long, long ago at rest. Still are thy pleasant voices, thy nightingales awake, for death he taketh all away but them he cannot take."

Veteran entertainer Johnny Beattie, who starred alongside Mr McKellar in many pantomimes and variety shows, also paid tribute.

Mr Beattie, star of BBC soap opera River City, recalled one of his last communications with the tenor, in which the actor suggested they write a musical version of that show.

"I can tell you that Ken was not amused," he said, to much laughter from the congregation.

He was   student at Aberdeen University, where his great singing voice first had a chance to shine.   Mr McKellar went on to take the world by storm as both an operatic tenor and a much-loved interpreter of Scottish songs.

But he wasn't always the confident performer, as yesterday's congregation at Paisley Abbey heard.

His daughter Jane told of a family occasion, recounted to her by the singer's brother Jimmy, when young Kenneth was just too shy to face his audience. "The only way he could do it was to turn and face the wall and sing," she said.

Mr McKellar died in April at the age of 82.

Yesterday's memorial service ended with a recording of him singing 'God Be In My Head' from the Book of Hours, followed by music from piper Ian McFadden, who played a medley of Scots songs, starting with another Burns favourite, 'Scots Wha Hae,' which remembers another famous son of Renfrewshire – Sir William Wallace.

Kenneth McKellar scholarship founded
Jul 12 2010 by Kenneth Speirs, Paisley Daily Express

A choral scholarship is to be set up in memory of legendary Scottish tenor Kenneth McKellar.

The Kenneth McKellar Memorial Scholarship will support a male chorister at Paisley Abbey – the church with which the singer had a close association for many years.

Born in Mary Street, Paisley, Mr McKellar had a worldwide reputation as a tenor and made a number of early recordings at the Abbey alongside organist and music director George McPhee.

Relatives of the popular singer – who died in April at the age of 82 – have announced they are to endow a scholarship worth £2,000 a year.

Dr McPhee said: "It will be for a scholarship with the choir and will be in conjunction with the Royal Scottish Academy of Music & Drama.

"The scholar will be probably be a tenor, but not necessarily, and will fulfil all the engagements of the choir on a Sunday.

The scholarship will be of mutual benefit to the Abbey and to the recipient, Dr McPhee added.

It will mean the church can be sure that it will have another skilled singer as part of the choir and give the scholar – who is likely to be a post-graduate music student – some choral experience.

It is expected that the first recipient of the scholarship, who will be chosen by Dr McPhee, will be announced later .

Appendix Part 1
'A Song for Everyone'

A Song for Everyone

Running Order
of
5 Programmes
Broadcast
on Radio Scotland

between 1954 and 1971

The author would like to acknowledge the assistance of BBC Scotland in providing   and allowing him to use the programme running orders for 'A Song for Everyone' in this part of the Appendix.

A Song for Everyone
Programme Running Order
First Broadcast 8th January 1954
with
Jack Nugent, Leader and Kenio Stephen, Conductor
BBC Scottish Variety Orchestra
Half Hour Long

1. 'Without a Song'
2. 'Answer Me'
3. 'My Love is Like a Red, Red Rose.'
4. 'The Flower Song'
5. 'Someday My Heart will Awake'
6. 'Fold Your Wings'
7. 'A Gordon for Me'
8. 'Where 'er You Walk'
9. 'The Road to the Isles'
10. 'Without a Song'

All items song by Kenneth McKellar except item 4 song by Barbara Leigh and item 5   a duet with Barbara Leigh and Kenneth McKellar

Script by   Eddie Boyd
Producer   Eddie Fraser

A Song for Everyone
Programme Running Order
First Broadcast 15th April 1958
with
Jack Leon
And the BBC Radio   Orchestra
This is the 100th Edition

One Hour Long

1. 'The Road to the Isles' sung by Kenneth McKellar
2. 'I'll Sing Thee Songs of Araby' by Kenneth McKellar
3. 'Voi Che Sapete'sung in English by Barbara Leigh
4. 'Phil the Fluters Ball'   by Kenneth McKellar
5. ' Fair Maid of Perth' by Kenneth McKellar
6. 'Joshua Fit De Battle of Jericho' sung by the Glasgow Police Male Voice Choir
7. 'Around the World' sung by Kenneth McKellar
8. 'Old Mother Hubbard' Sung by The Glasgow Police Male Voice Choir
9. 'Jacob and Bury' sung by Kenneth McKellar
10. ' Fold Your Wings' duet by Kenneth   McKellar and   Barbara Leigh
11. 'She Moved Through the Fair' sung by Kenneth McKellar

12. 'The Plough Boy' sung by Kenneth McKellar and accompanied by Alfred Furnish
13. 'O My Love is Like a Red, Red Rose' by Kenneth McKellar
14. 'The Cradle Song' sung by The Glasgow Police Male Voice Choir
15. 'You are My Hearts Desire ' sung by Kenneth McKellar
16. 'Annie Laurie' sung by Kenneth McKellar
17. 'When I grow too Old to Dream' sung by Barbara Leigh
18. 'Silent Worship' sung by Kenneth McKellar
19. 'Scotland the Brave' sung by Kenneth McKellar

Orchestra accompanied all items except item 12 and the Police Choir.
Producer   by Eddie Fraser
Script by Kenneth McKellar

A Song for Everyone
Programme Running Order
First Broadcast 27th June 1968
With
Iain Sutherland
and   the BBC Scottish Radio Orchestra

Half Hour Long

1. 'My Song'
2. 'The Tartan'
3. 'The Folks Who Live on the Hill'
4. 'My Heart and I'
5. 'Jeanie with the Light Brown Hair'
6. 'Sweet Charity'
7. 'Di miei Bollente Spiriti' sung in Italian
8. 'All the Things You Are'
9. 'The Garden Where the Praties Grow'
10 . 'My Love is Like a Red, Red Rose'
11. 'My Love is Like a Red, Red Rose'

All Items sung by Kenneth McKellar except Items 5 and
11 , by Orchestra.
The Producer is Eddie Fraser and the Script by
Kenneth McKellar.

'A Song For Everyone'
Programme running order
First Broadcast in 6th   April 1971
with
Iain Sutherland,
and the BBC Scottish Radio Orchestra
Order of Programme
Half Hour Programme

1.   'My Song'
2.   'The Thistle of Scotland'
3.   'Look to the Rainbow'
4.   'Your Eyes shine in My Own'
5.   'The Flower Song' (sung in English)
6.   'My Love is But a Lassie Yet'
7.   'O Surdato N'Amorato'
8.   'Every Time We Say Goodbye'
9.   'Dream Angus'
10. 'O My Love is Like a Red, Red Rose'
11. 'O My Love is Like a Red, Red Rose'

All Items sung by Kenneth McKellar except Item 6 and
11, by the Orchestra.

Producer   Eddie Fraser, who introduced the
programme.

Scrip by Kenneth McKellar

'A Song For Everyone'
Programme running order
First Broadcast in 1971
with
Brian Fahey, and the BBC Scottish Radio Orchestra
Order of Programme
Half Hour Programme

1. **'For Fame and For Fortune' by Jimmy Copland sung by Kenneth McKellar**
2. **'Dark Island' Sung by Kenneth McKellar**
3. **'Island Moon' by Duncan Morrison of Lewis sung by Morag McKay**
   from the Isle of Easdale in Argyll accompanied by her sister Rona on the harp.
4. **'Duros Dear' by Lady John Scott sung by Morag McKay.**
5. **'My Love is like a Red Red Rose' by Robert Burns sung by Kenneth   McKellar**
6. **'West Highland Way' sung by Kenneth McKellar**
7. **'The Crooked Bawbee' Duet with Morag McKay and Kenneth McKellar**
8. **'Annie Laurie' by Lady John Scott sung by Kenneth McKellar**

The programme was produced by Dave Batchelor.

Appendix 2   **Memorabilia**

Content
1. **Five Past Eight** - **Flyer**
2. **Five Past Eight** - **Programme**
3. **A Love for Jamie** - **Flyer**
4. **A Love for Jamie** - **Programme**
5. **This is Scotland** - **Flyer**
6. **This is Scotland** - **Programme**
7. **Gaiety Theatre** - **Programme Cover**
8. **Gaiety Theatre** - **Flyer Grand Re-opening**
9. **Gaiety Theatre** - **Programme Reopening - 1**
    (23rd April 1988)
10. **Gaiety Theatre** - **Programme Reopening - 2**
11. **Gaiety Theatre** - **Programme Cover**

12. **Gaiety Theatre** - **Flyer   Kenneth &**
Friends
13. **Gaiety Theatre** - **Programme**
    (15th May 1989)   **Kenneth & Friends**
14. **A Celebration of A Life - Part 1**
15. **A Celebration of A Life - Part 2**

Acknowledgements   to :

Items   1 to 4 The Glasgow Room
                Mitchell Library, Glasgow
Items 5 & 6   Paisley Reference Library

Items 7 to 13 Ayrshire Archives

Items 14 and 15   Paisley Daily Express

Memorabilia   for Kenneth McKellar

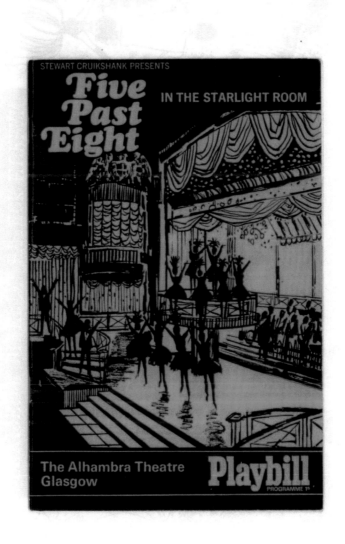

The Alhambra Theatre

Fabulous FIVE PAST EIGHT

OPENING OF A SHOW
(a) Light up the Sky .... The Geraldo Orchestra
(b) Theatre Street .... Peter Regan, Elaine Taylor,
The George Carden Dancers
and The Town Criers introduce
Rikki Fulton and Jack Milroy

(c) Startime .... Rikki

JUST RIKKI

CIRCUS IN TOWN
(a) Joey the Clown .. Peter Regan and Ensemble
(b) Cage of the Panthers .... Elaine Taylor with
Russ Arness and the Boys and Girls

HONEYMOONS OLD AND NEW
Jack, Ethel Scott, Glen Michael, Elaine

MUSIC FROM THE OPERA
Some of the music from Gounod's 'Faust',
sung by Gillian Humphreys
(from the D'Oyly Carte Opera Company)
with
Peter Regan and Vocal Ensemble

IT PAYS TO ADVERTISE .... Rikki

PARIS
(a) Champs Elysees .... Gillian Humphreys,
Peter Regan with the Ensemble
(b) Montmartre Introducing the "Living Screen"
devised and produced by Tony Tabacks
presented by arrangement with
The Tropicana Hotel, Las Vegas
(c) Folies Bergere .. Elaine Taylor, Russ Arness,
The Follies Girls
with
(d) The Ladies of Paree La Belle Fifi et Frou-Frou

The GERALDO Orchestra directed by BERKELEY SUTCLIFFE

COSTUMES DESIGNED by BERKELEY SUTCLIFFE

— INTERMISSION —

MUSIC A LA MODE
(a) Big Beat .... The Boys and Girls
(b) Operetta ... Gillian Humphreys and Ensemble

DR. JEKYLL'S CASEBOOK .... Rikki, Jack, Glen,
Clem, Ethel, Peter, Elaine and Bill

PAS DE DEUX .... Introducing
Belinda Wright and Jelko Yuresha
(by arrangement with the
Administrator, Royal Opera House, Covent Garden)

A TOUCH OF SCOTCH .... Jack

ROB MURRAY ... A Juggler—but only just!
direct from The Debbie Reynolds Show, Las Vegas

CLERICAL ERROR .... Rikki, Ethel, Glen,
Clem and Elaine

CABARET TIME
(a) Peter Regan with the Boys and Girls
(b) The Nutcracker Suite ... Belinda Wright and Jelko Yuresha
danced by Belinda Wright and Corps de Ballet
(choreography by Malcolm Goddard;
music arranged by Arthur Wilkinson;
and presented by permission of Bill Lyon-Shaw
and ABC Television)

TRAFFICATORS .... Rikki and Jack

FINALE .... The Full Company

DECOR by TOD KINGMAN

DEVISED & DIRECTED BY DICK HURRAN

DANCES STAGED BY DENNY BETTIS

The Five Past Eight Programme

ALHAMBRA THEATRE
GLASGOW

A LOVE FOR JAMIE

A STEWART CRUIKSHANK PRESENTATION

Kenneth McKellar
Rikki Fulton
Lenny the Lion (with Terry Hall)

DEVISED AND DIRECTED BY
FREDDIE CARPENTER

John Dick 1962

1/-
PLEASE SEE
THAT THIS
SEAL IS
UNBROKEN

PROGRAMME — ONE SHILLING

A Love for Jamie

Love for Jamie programme

OBAN CORRAN HALLS

8.30 MONDAYS, THURSDAYS

(Commencing 9th June, 1986)

DAVID WEBSTER of OBAN presents – IN PERSON

KENNETH McKELLAR

Scotland's Star Singer
in a night of Song and Dance live on stage

THIS IS SCOTLAND

Featuring, on the screen, an armchair tour through the
haunting beauty of the Scottish scene, photographed
and introduced by

DAVID WEBSTER of OBAN

MORAG MacINTYRE	★ PIPER TORQUIL TELFER ★	MURRAY MacKILLOP

SPECIAL GUEST – CHAMPION OF ARGYLL HIGHLAND DANCER
EILIDH MacINNES

Front Stalls : £3.85   Back Stalls : £3.45
OAPs: £3.35   Bairns: £2.35   OAPs: £2.95   Bairns: £1.95
Advance booking at the DAVID WEBSTER CAMERA CENTRE, corner Stafford & George
Street (Tel: Oban 63794) or at the CORRAN HALLS BOX OFFICE

Printed by R. M. Clunie & Co. Ltd. Oban

Poster for This is Scotland
Oban, Corran Halls

PROGRAMME

"This is Scotland"

1986 SUMMER SEASON

□ Please Note: Flash photography is NOT PERMITTED during the performance

THE NATIONAL ANTHEM

Piper TORQUIL TELFER
Scotland the Brave   Black Bear

Special Guest — Champion of Argyll Highland Dancer
EILIDH MacINNES

David Webster of Oban introduces . . . .
MORAG MACINTYRE . . . MURRAY MACKILLOP

EILIDH MACINNES with Piper TORQUIL TELFER
The Sword Dance

David Webster introduces the Voice of Scotland
KENNETH McKELLAR
with Scotland on the screen — photographed by
DAVID WEBSTER OF OBAN

Songs:
This is Scotland (Webster/Houliston)
Song of the Clyde Medley (Arr. McKellar)
The Royal Mile (McKellar/Gourlay)
West Highland Way (McKellar)
Oban My Home (Webster/Houliston)

As Day is Ended
TORQUIL TELFER

Highland Fling
EILIDH MacINNES

INTERVAL

CUT-PRICE COLOUR FILMS
110/24. £1.45 135/24. £1.45 135/36. £1.95
at the David Webster Camera Centre & Photo-Craft

SECOND HALF

Sailor's Hornpipe
EILIDH MACINNES

Piper
TORQUIL TELFER

KENNETH McKELLAR
with more scenes of Scotland photographed by
DAVID WEBSTER OF OBAN

Featuring songs old and new, from the Borders to the Highlands and
Islands, with visits to the Argyllshire Gathering in Oban and the
Cowal Games in Dunoon

Piper TORQUIL TELFER
Singalong: MORAG MACINTYRE and MURRAY MACKILLOP

KENNETH McKELLAR
WITH SOME MORE FAVOURITE SONGS
AULD LANG SYNE   NO AWA' TO BIDE AWA'

1—Persons shall not be permitted to stand or sit in any of the gangways intersecting the
   seating or sit in any of the other gangways

2—No Smoking is permitted in the auditorium

3—THE TAKING OF PHOTOGRAPHS IS NOT PERMITTED

4—No tape recorder or other type of recording apparatus may be brought into the
   auditorium

The management reserves the right to make any alteration in the performances which may
be rendered necessary by any unavoidable cause

Oban Corran Halls Programme

166

Ayr Gaiety Theatre Cover

Ayr Gaiety Theatre Programme

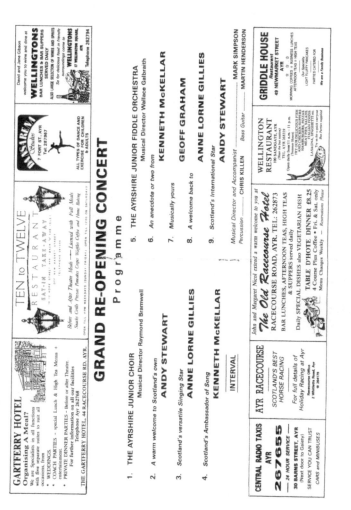

Ayr Gaiety Theatre Programme

Ayr Gaiety Programme Cover

Ayr Gaiety Theatre Programme

KENNETH McKELLAR AND FRIENDS

P r o g r a m m e

1. **A REEL WELCOME**
   International star piper GEORGE McILWHAM *with the*
   JIMMY COSKER TRIO

2. *Introducing Scotland's Own*
   KENNETH McKELLAR

3. *Popular Magical Comedian*
   JOHN SHEARER

4. *Violin Virtuoso*
   KAREN HUNTER

5. **JOHN SHEARER** *introduces*

6. *The lovely Scottish Singing Star*
   ANNE LORNE GILLIES

INTERVAL

7. GEORGE McILWHAM *"piper of pipers"*

8. JOHN SHEARER

9. KAREN HUNTER

10. *It's Magic*
    JOHN SHEARER

11. *International Television and recording Star*
    KENNETH McKELLAR
    at the piano MARK SIMPSON

12. THE COMPANY *wish you goodnight*

Ayr Gaiety Theatre Programme

A Celebration of the Life
of
Kenneth McKellar

30th June 2010
11.00am
Paisley Abbey, Scotland

Refreshments served in the North Transept, courtesy of Paisley Abbey.

With special thanks to:

The Reverend Alan Biss and the Paisley Abbey staff.
Councillor Celia Lawson, Provost of Renfrewshire.
Profesor George McPhee and the Paisley Abbey Choir
Joe Campbell, Ian Chapman, Johnny Beattie, Bill Hall
Rhona MacKay, Sonia Cromarty, Eddie McGuire
Walter Blair
Ian McFadden
Norman McCadie and Chilton Inglis

All donations to Paisley Abbey or to Cancer Research.

A Celebration of the Life

Traditional Airs - Musical arrangement by Kenneth McKellar
Trio: Rhona MacKay (harp); Sonia Cromarty (cello); Eddie McGuire (flute)

"Prayer to the Guardian Angel" (composed by Kenneth McKellar)
Paisley Abbey Choir, conducted by Professor George McPhee. Organ: Walter Blair

Reverend Alan Birss

Joe Campbell

"Ae Fond Kiss" – (Robert Burns)
Patricia Cahill & Kenneth McKellar

Ian Chapman

"Auld Lang Syne". (Robert Burns)
Tom Fleming

"The Holy City" – (Weatherly, Adams)
Kenneth McKellar and the Paisley Abbey Choir

Johnny Beattie

"In Paradisum" – (Fauré) –
Paisley Abbey Choir conducted by Professor George McPhee;
Harp - Rhona MacKay; Organ – Walter Blair

Bill Hall

"My Love is Like a Red Red Rose" – (Robert Burns)
Kenneth McKellar

Jane McKellar

"The Lost Chord" – (Arthur Sullivan)
Kenneth McKellar

Reverend Alan Birss

"God Be In My Head" – from the Book of Hours
Kenneth McKellar

Exit

Piper – Ian McFadden

A Celebration of the Life

Appendix Part 3

An Extract
from

The Kenneth McKellar
Song Book

20 Scottish Songs

(List of Songs on next page)

List of Songs

Granny's Heiland Hame
Mary of Argyll
The Bonnie Lass O' Ballochmyle
The Bluebells of Scotland
My Heart   is in the Highlands
Scots Wha' Hae
Loch Lomond
Land O' Hearts Desire
Ye Banks and Braes
Annie Laurie
The Long Ships
Kishmul's Galley
Westering Home
The Road to the Isles
The Mingulay Boat Song
Eriskay Love Lilt
The Northern Lights of Old Aberdeen
Aignish on the Machair
(Going West)
The Royal Mile
Mairi's Wedding

Permissions

Land o'Hearts Desire
The Long Ship
Kishmul's Galley
The Road to the Isles
An Eriskay Love Lilt
Aignish on the Machair
The above reproduced with permission of the copyright holder Boosey and Hawkes

Westering Home
The Mingulay Boat Song
The Lewis Boat Song
The above reproduced by permission of the copyright holder Roberton Publications

The Northern Lights of Old Aberdeen
The above reproduced   with the permission of the copyright holder Kerr's Music Corporation Limited

The Royal Mile
The above was reproduced with the permission of the copyright holder Francis Day and Hunter Limited

Granny's Heiland Hame

Away in the Heilands, there stands a wee hoose
And its stand on the breest o' the brae
Where we played as laddies there long, long ago
And it seems it was just yesterday
Chorus:
Where the heather bells are blooming
Just outside Granny's door
Where as laddies there we played
In days of long ago
Neath the shadow of Ben Bhraggie
And Golspie's lordly stane
How I wish that I could see
My Granny's heiland hame

I can still see old Granny, a smile on her face
Just as sweet as the heather dew
When I kissed her good bye, wi' a tear in her eye,
Said, laddie, may god bless you

In fancy again as I look o'er at Tain
When we played on the low Embro shore
From Dornoch to Scelbo, and roon by the mound
Was a ramble we'd take o'er and o'er

And oft times we'd play, near the old quarry brae
Where the laddies and lassies meet
And with old granny's smile, to cheer all the while
We'd stroll in our wee bare feet

Mary of Argyll

I have heard the mavis singing,
His love song to the morn,
I have seen the dew drop clinging,
To the rose just newly born.
But a sweeter song has cheer'd me,
At the ev'ning's gentle close,
And I've seen an eye still brighter.
Than the dew drop on the rose.
'Twas thy voice, my gentle Mary,
And thine artless winning smile,
That made this world an Eden.
Bonnie Mary of Argyll.

Tho' thy voice may lose its sweetness,
And thine eye its brightness too,
Tho' thy step may lack its fleetness,
And thy hair its sunny hue.
Still to me wilt thou be dearer,
Than all the world shall own,
I have loved thee for thy beauty,
But not for that alone.
I have watched thy heart, dear Mary,
And its goodness was the wile,
That has made thee mine forever.
Bonnie Mary of Argyll.

The Bonnie Lass O 'Ballochmyle

Fair is the morn in flow'ry May,
And sweet is night in autumn mild,
When roving thro' the garden gay,
Or wand'ring in the lonely wild;
But woman nature's darling child
There all her charms she does compile;
E'en there her other works are foil'd
E'en there her other works are foil'd
By the bonnie lass 0' Ballochmyle.
Chorus
The bonnie lass 0' Ballochmyle
The bonnie lass!
The bonnie, bonnie lass!
The bonnie lasso' Ballochmyle.

O had she been a country maid,
And I the happy country swain,
Tho' shelter'd in the lowest shed
That ever rose on Scotland's plain!
Thro' weary winter's wind and rain,
With joy, with rapture, I would toil;
And nightly to my bosom strain,
And nightly to my bosom strain,
The bonnie lass 0' Ballochmyle.
Chorus;
The bonnie lass 0' Ballochmyle
The bonnie lass!
The bonnie, bonnie lass!
The bonnie lass 0' Ballochmyle.
Oh where, tell me where, is your Highland laddie gone?

The Bluebells of Scotland

Oh where, tell me where, is your Highland laddie gone?
He's gone wi' streaming banners where noble deeds are done
And it's oh, in my heart I wish him safe at home

Oh where, tell me where, did your Highland laddie dwell?
Oh where, tell me where, did your Highland laddie dwell?
He dwelt in Bonnie Scotland, where blooms the sweet blue bell
And it's oh, in my heart I lo'ed my laddie well

Oh what, tell me what, does your Highland laddie wear?
Oh what, tell me what, does your Highland laddie wear?
A bonnet with a lofty plume, and on his breast a plaid
And it's oh, in my heart I lo'ed my Highland lad

Oh what, tell me what, if your Highland laddie is slain?
Oh what, tell me what, if your Highland laddie is slain?
Oh no, true love will be his guard and bring him safe again
For it's oh, my heart would break if my Highland lad were slain

My Hearts in the Highlands

Farewell to the Highlands, farewell to the North,
The birth-place of Valour, the country of Worth;
Wherever I wander, wherever I rove,
The hills of the Highlands for ever I love.

Chorus
My heart's in the Highlands, my heart is not here,
My heart's in the Highlands, a-chasing the deer;
Chasing the wild-deer, and following the roe,
My heart's in the Highlands, wherever I go.

Farewell to the mountains, high-cover'd with snow,
Farewell to the straths and green vallies below;
Farewell to the forests and wild-hanging woods,
Farewell to the torrents and loud-pouring floods.
Chorus

Scots Wha Hae

Scots, wha hae wi' Wallace bled,
Scots, wham Bruce has aften led,
Welcome to your gory bed,
Or to victorie.

Now's the day, and now's the hour;
See the front o' battle lour;
See approach proud Edward's pow'r,
Chains and slaverie!

Wha would be a traitor-knave?
Wha can fill a coward's grave?
Wha sae base as be a slave?
Let him turn and flie !

Wha for Scotland's king and law,
Freedom's sword will strongly draw,
Free-man stand, or free-man fa'?
Let him follow me.

By oppression's woes and pains!
By your sons in servile chains!
We will drain our dearest veins,
But they shall be free!

Lay the proud usurpers low!
Tyrants fall in ev'ry foe!
Liberty's in every blow!
Let us do - or die!!!

Loch Lomond

By yon bonnie banks and by yon bonnie braes,
Where the sun shines bright on Loch Lomond,
Where me and my true love were ever won't to gae
On the bonnie bonnie banks o' Loch Lomond

O' ye'll tak the high road and I'll tak the low road,
And I'll be in Scotland afore ye;
But me and my true love will never meet again,
On the bonnie bonnie banks o' loch Lomond

Twas there that we parted in yon shady glen,
On the steep steep side o' Ben Lomond,
Where in deep purple hue, the Hieland hills we view,
And the moon coming oot in the gloaming.

The wee birdies sing, and the wild flowers spring,
And in sunshine the waters are sleeping,
But the broken heart will ken nae second spring again,'
Though the waefu' may cease fae their greeting

Land O' Hearts Desire

Land O' Hearts desire ,
Isle of youth,
Dear Western Isle,
Gleaming in sunlight!
Land O' Heart's Desire
Isle of Youth!

Far the cloudless sky
Stretches blue
Across the Isle,
Green in the sunlight,
far the cloudless skye
Stretches blue.

There shall thou and I
wander free,
On sheen-white sands
Dreaming in starlight,
Land o' Hearts Desire
Isle of Youth.

Ye Banks and Braes

Ye banks and braes o' Bonnie Doon,
How can ye bloom sae fresh and fair?
How can ye chant, ye little birds,
And I'm sae weary, fu' o' care!

Ye'll break my heart, ye warbling birds,
That wanton through the flow'ring thorn
Ye mind me o' departed joys,
Departed, never to return.

Oft I have rove by bonnie doon,
To see the rose of woodbine twine;
And ilka bird sang of its love,
And fondly sae did I o' mine.

Wi' lightsome heart I put a rose,
Full sweet upon the thorny tree.
But my false lover stole my rose,
And ah, she left the thorn wi' me

Annie Laurie

Maxwelton's braes are bonnie
Where early fa's the dew
And 'twas there that Annie Laurie
Gave me her promise true.
Gave me her promise true
Which ne'er forgot will be
And for bonnie Annie Laurie
I'd lay me doon and dee.

Her brow is like the snowdrift
Her throat is like the swan
Her face it is the fairest
That e'er the sun shone on.
That e'er the sun shone on
And dark blue is her e'e
And for bonnie Annie Laurie
I'd lay me doon and dee.

Like dew on th'gowan lying
Is th' fa' o'her fairy feet
And like the winds in summer sighing
Her voice is low and sweet.
Her voice is low and sweet
And she's a' the world to me
And for bonnie Annie Laurie
I'd lay me doon and dee.

The Long Ships

Bend of arm and swing of shoulder
Cold the wind, but death is colder,
Hee-o-ho! Hee-o-ho! Hee-o-ho!

Blow of spume and crash of breaker
Ho ! Sword the orphan maker,
Hee-o-ho! Hee-o-ho! Hee-o-ho!

Bright the oar, the billow reaping
On the shore, the women weeping
Hee-o-ho! Hee-o-ho! Hee-o-ho!

Bend of keel, the land before us,
Thor and Odin hear our chorus,
Hee-o-ho! Hee-o-ho! Hee-o-ho!
Hear our chorus,Hee-o-ho! Hee-o-ho!

Kishmul's Galley

High from the Ben a Hayich
On a day of days,
Seaward I gaze,
Watching Kishmil's galley sailing.

Homeward she bravely battles
'Gainst the hurtling waves,
Not hoop nor yards,
Anchor, cable nor tackle has she

Now ar last'gainst wind and tide,
They've brought her to
'Neath Kishmul's walls,
Kishmul Castle, our ancient glory.

Here's red wine and feast for heroes
And harping too,
Sweet harping too.

Westering Home

Tell me o' lands o' the Orient gay,
Sing o' the riches and joys o' Cathay
Man! But it's grand to awaken each day
And find yourself nearer to Isla.

Chorus
Westering home wi' a song in the air
Light in me heart an' it's goodbye to care
Laughter o' love and a welcomin' there
Isle o' me heart, me own land.

Wha' are the folks like the folks o' the west?
Canty an' couthy an' kind to the best
There I would lay me and there I would rest
At home wi' my ain folks at Isla.
Chorus

The Road to the Isles

A far croonin' is pullin' me away
As take I wi' my cromak to the road.
The far Coolins are puttin' love on me
As step I wi' the sunlight for my load.

Chorus:
Sure, by Tummel and Loch Rannoch and Lochaber I
will go.
By heather tracks wi' heaven in their wiles;
If it's thinkin' in your inner heart braggart's in my step,
You've never smelt the tangle 0' the Isles.
Oh, the far Coolins are puttin' love on me.
As step I wi' my cromak to the Isles.

It's by Sheil water and track is to the west.
By Aillort and by Morar to the sea,
The cool cresses I am thinkin' o' for pluck,
And bracken for a wink on Mother knee.

Chorus: Sure, by Tummel etc.

It's the blue Islands are pullin' me away,
Their laughter puts the leap upon the lame,
The blue Islands from the Skerries to the Lews,
Wi' heather honey taste upon each name.

Chorus: Sure, by Tummel etc.

Mingulay Boat Song

Chorus
Hill yo ho, boys; let her go, boys;
Bring her head round, into the weather,
Hill you ho, boys; let her go, boys
Sailing homeward to Mingulay

What care we though, white the Minch is?
What care we for wind or weather?
Let her go boys; every inch is
Sailing homeward to Mingulay.
Chorus

Wives are waiting, by the pier head,
Or looking seaward, from the heather;
Pull her round, boys, then you'll anchor
'Ere the sun sets on Mingulay.
Chorus

Ships return now, heavy laden
Mothers holdin' bairns a-cryin'
They'll return, though, when the sun sets
They'll return to Mingulay.
Chorus

Eriskay Love Lilt

Chorus
Vair me o, ro van o
Vair me o ro ven ee,
Vair me o ru o ho
Sad I am without thee.

When I'm lonely, dear white heart,
Black the night and wild the sea;
By love's light my foot finds
The old pathway to thee.

Chorus

Thou'rt the music of my heart,
Harp of joy, o cuit mo chridh,
Moon of guidance by night,
Strength and light thou'rt to me.

Northern Lights Of Old Aberdeen

When I was a lad, a tiny wee lad
My mother said to me
Come see the Northern Lights my boy
They're bright as they can be
She called them the heavenly dancers
Merry dancers in the sky
I'll never forget, that wonderful sight
They made the heavens bright

Chorus:
The Northern Lights of old Aberdeen
Mean home sweet home to me
The Northern Lights of old Aberdeen
Are what I long to see
I've been a wanderer all of my life
Any many a sight I've seen
God speed the day when l' m on my way
To my home in Aberdeen

I've wandered in many far-off lands
And travelled many a mile
I've missed the folk I cherished most
The joy of a friendly smile
It warms up the heart of a wand'rer
The clasp of a welcoming hand
To greet me when, I return
Home to my native land
Chorus

Aignish on the Machair

When   day and night are over,
And the world is done with me,
Oh, carry me West and lay me
In Aignish, Aignish by the sea

And never heed my lying,
Among the ancient dead,
Beside the white sea breakers
And sand-drift overhead.

The grey gulls wheeling over,
And the wide arch of the sky,
O Aignish, Aignish on the Machair,
Be quiet, quiet there to lie,
Be quiet, quiet there to lie.

The Royal Mile

If fate decreed that I could walk just one mile each day,
And I with age and sorrows weighed were giv'n my choice of way,
I'd choose from ev'ry mile I've crossed on land or sea or air,
The mile that makes a Scotsman proud of Edinburgh's fair.

Chorus
O   let me walk the Royal Mile, that's Scotland's brave highway;
Where at one o'clock from the castle rock comes 'Auld Reekie's' call each day,
And as the echo sounds in the palace grounds,
Then the Heav'ns on Scotland smile,
And you've made your day in a royal way on the Royal Mile,
Yes you've made your day in a royal way on the Royal Mile.

When I walked the famous mile the air about me rings
With footsteps made in years gone by,   by princes , queens and kings,
For here is Scotland's history, here freedom lost and won,
And here my heart is ever homing, 'til my life is done.

Chorus

Mairi's wedding

Chorus
Step we gaily on we go
Heel for heel and toe for toe
Arm in arm and row and row
All for Mairi' s wedding

Over hill-way up and down
Myrtle green and bracken brown
Past the shieling through the town
All for Mairi's wedding
Chorus

Plenty herring plenty meal
Plenty peat tae fill her creel
Plenty bonny bairns as weel
That's the toast for Mairi
Chorus

Cheeks as bright as rowans are
Brighter far than any star
Fairest of them all by far is my darling Mairi
Chorus

Over hill-ways up and down
Myrtle green and bracken brown
Past the sheiling through the town
All for sake of Mairi
Chorus

Bibliography

Bowditch, Lynditch
Robert Burns Birthplace Museum
National Trust for Scotland   2010

Clayson, Alan
The Very Best of Kenneth Mckellar
(CD notes)
Karusell International 1997

Fulton Rikki
'Is It That Time Already?
Black and White Publishing , 1999

Grigor, Robbie
Just Daft, The Chic Murray Story
Birlinn Limited, 2008

Horricks, Raymond
Kenneth McKellar, The Decca Years 1955 - 1975
(CD Notes)
The Decca Record Company Limited 1999

Irving, Gordon
The Good Auld Days
Jupiter Books (London) Limited 1977

Moore, John
The Gaiety,
South Ayrshire Council

McKellar, Kenneth
The Songs of Robert Burns
(CD note)
Vocalion, 2004

McKellar, Kenneth
The Romantic Scotland of Kenneth McKellar,
Jarrold Colour Publications